W.S.C.
A CARTOON BIOGRAPHY

W.S.C.
A CARTOON
BIOGRAPHY

COMPILED BY
FRED URQUHART

WITH A FOREWORD BY
HAROLD NICOLSON

CASSELL & COMPANY LTD
LONDON

CASSELL & CO LTD
37/38 St. Andrew's Hill, Queen Victoria Street,
London, E.C.4
and at

31/34 George IV Bridge, Edinburgh; 210 Queen Street, Melbourne; 26/30 Clarence Street, Sydney; Uhlmann Road, Hawthorne, Brisbane; C.P.O. 3031, Auckland, N.Z.; 1068 Broadview Avenue, Toronto 6; P.O. Box 275, Cape Town; P.O. Box 1386, Salisbury, S. Rhodesia; Munsoor Building, Main Street, Colombo 11; Haroon Chambers, South Napier Road, Karachi; 13/14 Ajmeri Gate Extension, New Delhi; 15 Graham Road, Ballard Estate, Bombay 1; 17 Chittaranjan Avenue, Calcutta 13; Avenida 9 de Julho 1138, São Paulo; Galeria Güemes, Escritorio 518/520 Florida 165, Buenos Aires; P.O. Box 959, Accra, Gold Coast; 25 rue Henri Barbusse, Paris 5e; Islands Brygge 5, Copenhagen.

First published March 1955
All rights reserved

920
C563u

113007

Printed in Great Britain by
*Lowe and Brydone (Printers) Limited, London, N.W.*10
F.1154

To the great man

who is the subject of the

following pages

ACKNOWLEDGEMENTS

For permission to reproduce the drawings in this book the publishers wish to express their gratitude to the proprietors of the newspapers and journals in which these cartoons first appeared. A special word of thanks is due to Dr. Martin Hürlimann, The Institut Français, The Institute of Italian Culture, The Library of the American Embassy, Odhams Press Limited, and The Wiener Library for their assistance in gathering together the present collection.

CONTENTS

FOREWORD
by HAROLD NICOLSON viii

LIST OF SOURCES xii

LIST OF ARTISTS xiii

THE CARTOONS 1

FOREWORD

by HAROLD NICOLSON

EVER since the stone age, man has used the device of caricature both as a branch of artistic creation and as a weapon of invective or ridicule. Great artists—such as Goya, Hogarth and Daumier—have experimented in this medium, and it has furnished agreeable exercise to such gifted draftsmen as Gavarni, Caran d'Ache, Charles Dana Gibson and Phil May. In England, the gross but brilliant diatribes of Gillray, Rowlandson and Cruikshank were succeeded during the Victorian age by the gentler manner of Leech, Tenniel and Gould. Caricatures ceased to be distortions of the human figure and became, in the hands of men like Bernard Partridge, flattering portraits of statesmen at their noblest. In more recent years, I am glad to say, David Low and Vicky have done much to reintroduce into our cartoons something of the old eighteenth-century vigour of derision.

Although for the student of the subject there stretch several centuries of English political caricature to which he can devote his industry and researches, it is rarely indeed that a single statesman becomes prominent so young and remains prominent for so many decades that we can study the development of caricature in a highly concentrated personal form. The present collection of kind or unkind drawings of Winston Churchill covers more than half a century. Whatever may have been the storms and whirlwinds which he endured and in the end directed, he remains throughout a most individual, intimate, lovable and provocative human being, whom the gods have delighted to abase and to honour and whom the caricaturists for the last fifty-five years have delighted to draw.

It is interesting, for instance, to observe that there is always a time-lag between the date when the features of a politician become generally recognizable and recognized and the date when they assume what might be called standard caricatural form. In earlier periods, before the camera had come to snap our celebrities in their most informal postures and moments, this time-lag was prolonged. Thus Gillray continued to portray Bonaparte as a lean wild Jacobin many years after he had settled down to his rotund and seemingly placid consular shape. In our own days, also, it took the caricaturists much time and trouble before they invented the proper formula for Stanley Baldwin. That quiet statesman possessed no marked eccentricity of feature ; in the end the caricaturist had to exploit the constant pipe and to make the very most of the hitherto unnoticed indentations of his nose. The Baldwin formula, once invented, remained stable until the end of his life. The Lloyd George formula also took some time to come into its own. The early caricatures represent him as a haggard and dishevelled agitator waving arms : it was Low, I think, who first caught the vivacious, the almost startled, expression of his eyes. Thereafter Lloyd George was always depicted with eyebrows raised in animation, excitement, amusement or rage. It was not a bad formula.

Winston Churchill also, in his younger years, possessed no predominant feature such as might facilitate the caricaturist's art. The bull-dog expression with which we now associate his portraits did not develop until defeats, misrepresentations and power had come to steel his pugnacity and fortify his will. Compare, for instance, the Spy drawing which figures as the first illustration in this volume with the dazzling sketch made by Low twenty-six years later. My own early memories of Winston Churchill date from 1906 and I can detect no resemblance at all between those memories and the likeness caught by Spy. The clothes are correct, the wing collar and bow tie are such as I recall them, and there is that old-fashioned watch chain which glistens to this day across the black waistcoat. There is a touch about the mouth and cheeks which suggests resemblance, but the nose, the eyes and the hair are those, not of the young Churchill, but of some other man. When we turn to Low, however, we are immediately in the orbit of recognition. The eyes are there, poised before the moment of explosion, the nature of which still remains uncertain. Is this vivid figure about to say something very amusing or very rude ? Low has caught the smoulder in the eyes, when the observer knows that the faint eyelids will in a second or two be raised for an expletive, which may be pungent but which may be just schoolboy fun. It needs an artist of Low's vivid memory and execution to convey the unpredictable Churchill ;—those sudden moments when sullen brooding flashes into alert attention. Churchill is about to spring.

It is fascinating also, as we turn the pages of this collection, to observe the successive symbols, adjuncts or properties which the caricaturists employed. When Churchill was escaping from Pretoria across the veldt he was accompanied by a vulture, who settled with patient appetite at a short distance from where he crouched and hid. This bird, for a year or two, caught the fancy of the caricaturists and thereafter became so irrelevant that today we can scarcely see the point. There then followed a prolonged period when Winston Churchill was invariably depicted as wearing a new variety of little hat. I do remember vaguely that his hats were often too small for his majestic brow and gave the impression that they had perched rather than settled. Yet long after the head-gear of Churchill had ceased to be eccentric or even remarkable the caricaturists continued to place the hats of sailors or schoolchildren tiny upon the dome of his head.

It was many years before the hat-symbol was replaced by the cigar-symbol which has remained the most customary of all the properties. It figures delightfully in Osbert Lancaster's drawing of January 1943 in which Winston Churchill is depicted as visiting the Casablanca conference disguised as a Moorish matron, complete with yashmak and ewer. From under the veil there protrudes the cigar. " Well," exclaims a citizen of Casablanca to his neighbour, " if it isn't the widow Fatima, who is it ? Just tell me that ! " Even in the German and Italian caricatures of the second war the cigar is added as a means of identification and a hint of self-indulgence. Gradually also the caricaturists introduce into the pictures allusions to Churchill's special hobbies. The brick-laying period is not very prolonged, but often the statesman is represented as sadly building walls. The painting theme figures increasingly. During the lonely gap which ended only after the collapse of Munich illusions, the easel is as constant a companion as the vulture ever was and it becomes a symbol of increasing popular sympathy and affection. There follows the triumphant period of the V sign, that odd little Churchillian quirk, and in the end there is the note of apotheosis when the great man is depicted strutting happily in Garter robes.

These are the lighter sides which this collection discloses. Its more serious aspects remind us of the gales of political unpopularity and suspicion which Churchill has had to brave. We today regard him as established for ever in our national Valhalla. It is salutary to be reminded how bitter were the animosities, how dark the lies, how almost unendurable the injustices which, until 1940, he had constantly to endure. Today, when we look back across those fifty years, when we consult not our own feelings and evidence only but the opinions of our former enemies, we realize that even in the transactions that were held as errors against him his vision was correct. Over those of his impulses which can still be cited as errors of judgment, there is today a light shining of romance. He may have been wrong in the attitude he took over the India Act and the Abdication ; but his defiance of contemporary opinion on such occasions was not due to any egoism or self-advantage but to an overpowering loyalty to lost causes or stricken friends. For us they shine happily today as myrtle flowers among the heavy wreath of bay.

As we examine this scrap-book we can detect some seven successive phases in the public estimate of Winston Churchill. There is the early conception of him as the gay young soldier, the man who before he was twenty-five had seen five different campaigns and written brilliantly about all of them. There then follows the short period of his first entry into Parliament, when the caricaturists saw in him the image of his dazzling father. It must be confessed that the young Member for Oldham did little to discourage this identification. He dressed as his father had dressed ; he occupied his father's old seat on the benches ; he reflected his father's stance and manner of oratory ; and the dynamic brilliance of Lord Randolph lived again in the ebullience of his obstreperous red-headed son. It was quickly realized that the young Churchill was no respecter of the venerable or the imposing.

It only took the observers in the reporters' gallery a few short months to realize that this new Churchill was no mere imitation of his father, but a dynamo in himself. They began to suggest that he was a little too buoyant ; that he was lacking in the modesty that older men always assert to be so recommendable in the young. " The duties," he is represented as murmuring, " of confidential adviser to Lord Roberts are not light." E. T. Read shows him yelling like a naughty Harrovian at the flustered figure of Sir Trout Bartley ; in a careful cartoon Bernard Partridge marks the difference between the staid Lord Elgin and his dashing Parliamentary Under Secretary in terms of a panathenaic frieze. It is in this cartoon, incidentally, that Churchill sheds the schoolboy manner and becomes the public figure so familiar to us in subsequent drawings.

From his earliest days Churchill possessed what is known as " news value ". There is a revealing cartoon by Raven Hill, dated 1913, which shows Asquith and Churchill yachting in the *Enchantress* together in the Mediterranean. The papers have come on board and Asquith opens them, while Churchill is stretched in a deck chair beside him. " Any news ? " asks the younger man. " How can there be," replies Asquith, " with you here ? "

Although he became a public figure before he was thirty, the young Churchill fascinated rather than impressed his fellows. He was regarded as restless, reckless, too daring, far too versatile. The several variations in his party allegiances caused disquiet. The British public prefer to know where they stand ; with Churchill you were never sure what he would do next. His energy caused them uneasiness ; his imaginative sallies inspired dismay. He was considered brilliant rather than sound ; the British have always preferred sedatives to stimulants ; Churchill was regarded as lacking in constancy and judgment.

There followed the prolonged period when he was viewed with distrust. He was not at any stage of his life an equable person and among his many virtues has never been numbered that of suffering fools with gladness or even calm. The Sidney Street episode, when as Home Secretary he personally faced the bullets of anarchists, was not at the time viewed as a delightful manifestation of courage. It was thought unseemly. The threatened rebellion in Ulster, which he took steps to forestall or if necessary to combat, was the occasion of much animosity against him. And then, with the first war, came the Dardanelles failure, the quarrel with Lord Fisher, and the collapse of his repute. We now know the injustice of these criticisms ; the strategic plan was correct and had it been carried out with tactical vigour it might have shortened the war by two years and perhaps even have prevented the Russian revolution from taking so destructive a form. Yet the entire blame for these misfortunes was laid on Churchill's shoulders. He resigned his office and went off to fight in the trenches with the younger men.

It is salutary, if painful, to glance for a moment at the Low cartoo . which appeared on January 21st, 1920 ; it is reproduced on page 39 of this album. Churchill is shown in a napoleonic pose with the dead cats of his misfortunes lying at his feet, and labelled " Gallipoli Mistake", " Antwerp Blunder ", " Sidney Street ", " Russian Bungle ". His initiative in these matters had not been mistaken ; yet for years he had to endure these imputations and for years they hampered and delayed the full fruition of his vision and strength.

Then came the second world war and Churchill ceases suddenly to be the disturber of peace, the author of wildcat schemes, and becomes the bulwark of our fortitude, the pilot in the typhoon, the father of victory. The V sign comes to join the cigar as a symbol and in the end we have the Grand Old Man, smiling impishly in Garter robes, and reducing all critics and competitors to the proportion of little ants crawling around his shoes. Thus we have Strube's cartoon of November 1953 with History stretching out the wreath of triumph to an array of all the varied Churchills of the past. Stretched above this joyful procession is a hand making a gigantic V sign against the sky. The last caricature in this album depicts Churchill as an amicable bull-dog arrayed in an ordinary bowler hat. It is a sedative picture and makes a pleasant epilogue to the life of a man who has aroused much hatred in his time and who at the end knows himself to be surrounded by the gratitude of all good men.

I trust that readers will derive, from this illustrated catalogue of half a century of abuse, the comforting reflection that, if one's character be sturdy and one's principles be solid, one can look back upon such diatribes with the satisfaction derived from disappointments heroically endured and triumphs accepted as benedictions.

LIST OF SOURCES

The numbers indicate the pages on which the cartoons appear

ACTION, PARIS, 179, 182

BHARAT JYOTI, BOMBAY, 227, 228

BIRMINGHAM EVENING DESPATCH, 12

CARREFOUR, PARIS, 172

CHICAGO TRIBUNE, 148, 150, 151, 157, 158

CHRISTIAN SCIENCE MONITOR, BOSTON, 156

CIVIL AND MILITARY GAZETTE, LAHORE, 88, 107, 122

COURIER, 132, 139, 141, 171, 181

DAGBLADET, OSLO, 180

DAILY EXPRESS, 24, 28, 29, 30, 36, 37, 40, 44, 47, 48, 56, 62, 64, 66, 70, 74, 75, 82, 84, 105, 130, 134, 172, 204, 218, 226, 231, 237, 238

DAILY HERALD, 27, 97, 185, 186, 187, 188, 192, 197, 199, 205, 209

DAILY MAIL, 35, 38, 41, 46, 49, 50, 52, 59, 62, 63, 64, 65, 67, 68, 76, 77, 103, 104, 110, 111, 112, 116, 119, 120, 123, 127, 130, 137, 144, 154, 159, 165, 166, 175, 183

DAILY MIRROR, 100, 106, 117, 124, 140, 149, 236, 240

DAILY WORKER, 173, 182, 184, 190, 195, 212, 213, 215, 216, 221, 223

DAS SCHWARZE KORPS, MUNICH, 142, 143

DE GROENE AMSTERDAMMER, 101

DE MISTHOORN, AMSTERDAM, 115

DER STURMER, NUREMBERG, 98, 102, 113, 114, 126

DUBLIN OPINION, 167

EVENING NEWS, 31

EVENING STANDARD, 83, 85, 125, 170

FIFTY CARICATURES, 14

'420', FLORENCE, 108

FRANC-TIREUR, PARIS, 224

FREE PRESS JOURNAL, BOMBAY, 219

FRONT NATIONAL, PARIS, 160

HIRDMANNEN, OSLO, 115

IL MONDO, ROME, 191

IL TRAVASO, ROME, 239, 242

ISKUSTVO, MOSCOW, 208

KLADDERADATSCH, BERLIN, 98

KROKODIL, MOSCOW, 200, 201, 202

LA FRANCE, PARIS, 159

LE FIGARO, PARIS, 230

LE PETIT PARISIEN, 138

MANCHESTER DAILY DISPATCH, 135, 145, 147, 153, 155

MANCHESTER GUARDIAN, 220, 225, 234

MARC' AURELIO, ROME, 109

MELBOURNE ARGUS, 95

NATAL DAILY NEWS, 109

NEWS CHRONICLE, 130, 160, 162, 164, 169, 177, 178, 179, 189, 193, 194, 196, 203, 206, 207, 210, 211, 214, 222, 232, 235, 241, 242

NEWS OF THE WORLD, 118

NEW REPUBLIC, NEW YORK, 176

NEW STATESMAN, 71

NEW YORK DAILY MIRROR, 129

PHILADELPHIA INQUIRER, 92

PRAVDA, MOSCOW, 198

PUNCH, 2, 5, 6, 7, 9, 10, 11, 15, 16, 17, 19, 20, 22, 23, 25, 32, 33, 34, 35, 42, 48, 51, 57, 69, 81, 86, 87, 89, 128

RAND DAILY MAIL, 180

REPORTER, NEW YORK, 217

REYNOLD'S ILLUSTRATED NEWS, 72, 73, 78, 79, 80, 81

REYNOLDS NEWS, 195, 202

REYNOLDS'S NEWSPAPER, 19, 31, 49, 53, 55

ST. LOUIS POST-DISPATCH, 174

SIMPLICISSIMUS, MUNICH, 91, 93, 94, 99

STAR, 39, 43, 45, 54, 58, 60, 61, 69

SUNDAY EXPRESS, 146, 233

SUNDAY TIMES, 229

TATLER, 18

THE BALFOURIAN PARLIAMENT, 2

THE END OF A TALE : A TRIBUTE TO POY, 121, 131

THE HAGUE POST, 96

TIME AND TIDE, 114, 129, 131, 168

TRIBUNE, 88, 90, 131, 133, 136, 152, 163

VANITY FAIR, 1

VOELKISCHER BEOBACHTER, BERLIN, 95

WESTMINSTER GAZETTE, 3, 4, 8, 13, 21, 26

WORLD'S PRESS NEWS, 161

LIST OF ARTISTS

The numbers indicate the pages on which the cartoons appear

ANDERSON, 152
BARTOLI, A., 191
BEERBOHM, MAX, 14, 18, 48
BELLI, E., 239
BERG, MITEL, 179
BERGER, 118, 141, 171
BLI, 180
BROOK, RICARDO, 48
BURIKO, 108
BUTTERWORTH, 135, 145, 147, 153, 154
CARMACK, 156
CARSTAIRS, J. L., 85
CHALLEN, 88, 90
CONNELLY, 180
COTTERALL, TOM, 56
CUMMINGS, 218, 226, 231, 237
CURRY, 224
DERRICK, THOMAS, 168
DYSON, WILL, 27
EFFEL, JEAN, 160, 172
EMMWOOD, 233
EPHEMOVA, V., 201
FIPS, 98, 102, 113, 114, 126
FITZPATRICK, 174
FRIELLE, 195, 202
GABRIEL, 173, 182, 184, 190, 195, 212, 213, 215, 216, 221, 223
GARVENS, 98
G.E.K., 167
GILES, 134, 146, 204
GOULD, F. CARRUTHERS, 3, 4, 8, 13, 21, 26
GULBRANSSON, OLAF, 91
HOLLAND, FRANK, 19, 31, 53, 55
HORNER, 232, 235, 241
HUTTON, 92
ILLINGWORTH, 103, 104, 110, 111, 112, 116, 119, 120, 123, 127, 128, 137, 144, 154, 165, 166, 175, 183
KEM, 138
KRAUB, ROBERT, 143
KRAUS, 142
KRR, 115
KUKRINIKSI, 198, 208
LAMBDA, 136
LANCASTER, OSBERT, 130

LEYDEN, 109
LLOYD, A. W. (A. W. LL.), 35, 42, 69, 81, 85
LOW, 39, 43, 45, 54, 58, 60, 61, 69, 71, 83, 85, 125, 170, 181, 197, 199, 205, 209, 220, 225, 234
MULALLY, 163
MUNRO, 88, 107, 122
NARET, JACQUES, 182
NEB, 130, 159
NELSON, RAPHAEL, 114
PARRISH, 150, 157, 158
PARTRIDGE, BERNARD, 9, 22
POY, 31, 35, 38, 41, 46, 49, 50, 59, 62, 63, 64, 65, 67, 68, 76, 77, 121, 131
RAVENHILL, L., 16, 17, 23, 51, 57
REED, E. T., 2, 5, 6, 7, 9, 10, 11, 15, 19, 20
SCHILLING, ERICH, 99
SCHLOSS, E., 176
SCHULTZ, WILHELM, 94
SENNEP, 230
SHEPARD, E. H., 87, 89
SIMS, ARTHUR, 217
SOMDAL, CARL, 148, 151
SPENCER, WILL, 242
SPI, 72, 73, 79, 80
SPY, 1
STEPHEN, 139
STRUBE, 24, 28, 29, 30, 36, 37, 40, 44, 47, 62, 64, 66, 70, 74, 75, 82, 84, 105, 172, 229
THACKERAY, 219, 227, 228
THORNY, E., 93
TIM, 161
TITT, TOM, 49
TOWNSEND, F. H., 25, 32, 33, 34
ULLYETT, ROY, 238
VAKSENOVA, A., 202
VALKA, G., 200
VICKY, 129, 130, 131, 160, 162, 164, 169, 177, 178, 179, 189, 193, 194, 196, 203, 206, 207, 210, 211, 214, 222, 236, 240
WEBSTER, TOM, 132
WHITELAW, GEORGE, 97, 185, 186, 187, 188, 192
WOOD, 131, 133
ZEC, 100, 106, 117, 124, 140, 149

While acting as War Correspondent in the South African War, young Winston Churchill was captured by the Boers. He made a sensational escape, became a National Figure, and returned to England to stand as Conservative candidate for Oldham in the " Khaki " Election of September 1900. This caricature by Spy appeared just before the election beside an article " Men of the Day : No. DCCXCII " by Jehu Junior, who wrote : " He can write and he can fight . . . He is something of a sportsman ; he prides himself on being practical rather than a dandy ; he is ambitious ; he means to get on, and he loves his country. But he can hardly be the slave of any party."

The Balfourian Parliament (1906)
Cartoon by E. T. Reed, 1901

Churchill won the election with a majority of 230 votes and received a telegram of congratulations from Lord Salisbury, the Conservative Prime Minister. Before taking his seat in Parliament in February 1901, the first Parliament of King Edward VII, he went on a lecture tour of England and U.S.A.

SON AND FATHER

Winston Churchill made his maiden speech on 18th February 1901. His greatest admiration at this period was reserved for his father, who died at the age of forty-five in 1895, and he spent the time not occupied by Parliamentary duties in writing his biography, *Lord Randolph Churchill*, which was published in 1905.

MR. BRODRICK AND MR. WINSTON CHURCHILL

AN UNCOMFORTABLE NEIGHBOUR

During his escape in South Africa, Winston had been plagued by a
vulture. Mr. Brodrick, who had been inimical to Lord Randolph, was
Minister of War in the present Government, and when young Winston
criticized Mr. Brodrick's Army Expansion and pleaded the cause of
economy in Parliament, Mr. Brodrick realized that the tables were being
turned.

WHIPPING THEM UP

A " four-line " whip had been sent out by Sir William Walrond, the chief Ministerial Whip, urging the Government need of increased support from its followers.

(Misled by the term " whipping " a French provincial journal some time ago solemnly related as a fact that when Members of Parliament grew slack in the support of their party, an official called on them with a big whip, which he cracked threateningly and then marched them down to the House. The above drawing shows how Caran d'Ache would probably treat the present situation. Sir William Walrond is shown personally conducting Mr. Bowles, Mr. Bartley and Mr. Winston Churchill.)

Back-benchers are expected to obey the Party Whips. But if they are ambitious, critical and rebels, this is sometimes difficult to do. During his first years in Parliament, young Churchill found it increasingly hard to toe the Party "line", and as time went on he gradually became a Radical.

" Yes, men of Oldham."

" It never got over my escape."

" The duties of confidential adviser
to Lord Roberts are not light."

" That's how I fetch Oldham."

These four cartoons illustrated an article in *Punch*, in which the young Member for Oldham was found in front of a mirror, rehearsing a speech for his constituents.

WINSTON AND SIR TROUT

(A STUDY IN DEPORTMENT)

Churchill became more Radical, and he often roused his Conservative fellows to fury. In March 1904 his close friend, Major Seely, resigned from the Conservative Party on the question of "Chinese slavery" in South Africa. There was such an outcry that Major Seely could scarcely make himself heard, and Churchill shouted above the din : " I am quite unable to hear what my honourable Friend is saying owing to the vulgar clamour maintained by the Conservative Party." At this, Sir Trout Bartley shouted that " the vulgarest expression came from this honourable Gentleman". On 31st May Mr. Churchill crossed the House and took his seat on the Liberal benches beside Lloyd George.

THE WANKLYN

" I absolutely decline to regard Mr. Churchill as being on the earth.   I ignore him utterly."

(DAILY MIRROR *interview with Mr. W-nkl-n, M.P.*)

Mr. J. L. Wanklyn, a Tory M.P., accused Winston Churchill of having played with the idea of wresting the leadership from Arthur Balfour (the Prime Minister) as far back as 1902, and of establishing a weak Radical Ministry under his own leadership.   Churchill denied this, and the controversy which took place in the columns of *The Times* of this date makes amusing reading.   While at Harrow, young Winston won the Public Schools fencing championship.

MUTUAL ATTENTIONS

Mr. Winston Churchill : *It reminds me of that confounded bird that haunted me on the veldt !*

(*Mr. Winston Churchill some time since declared his intention to keep his eye on Mr. Chamberlain. Mr. Chamberlain is keeping his eye on Mr. Winston Churchill.*)

In 1905 Winston Churchill became Under-Secretary for the Colonies in the first Liberal Government for ten years, under the Premiership of Sir Henry Campbell-Bannerman.

AN ELGIN MARBLE

Bas-relief in the manner of the Parthenon Frieze (commonly called the Elgin Marbles). Design attributed to Mr. W-nst-n Ch-rch-ll.

Lord Elgin, the Colonial Secretary, sat in the House of Lords, so this gave his Under-Secretary more scope in the House of Commons.

THE LATEST DELICACY AT THE " CARLTON "

" Repatriation (in the New Hebrides) had peculiar difficulties . . . It was like repatriating the Under-Secretary for the Colonies to the other side (Laughter). If they popped him down on one side of the island he was admired, respected, and cheered ; but on the other side he was eaten (Loud laughter)."—(Sir Ch-rl-s D-lke's speech).

According to *Punch*, Mr. Weir, a Scottish M.P., was surprised to hear the House discussing Labour questions in the New Hebrides (prompted by a speech by Sir Charles Dilke). He did not like the adjective. As far as he was concerned, there was only one Hebrides. Hunger was often known in the islands of Uist and Lewis, but the Scots stopped short at cannibalism.

MORE TELEPATHY AT WESTMINSTER

MR. B-LF-R (lightly touching the cranium of C.-B.) : " *Now this?   What have I here ?* "

MR. L-TT-LT-N : " *You have there a Scotchman of great humour ; he comes from Stirling ; he has a profound desire for peace—with some people ; he detests slavery—in some places.   What is he thinking of ?—The House of Lords.*"

MR. B. : " *Now this ?* "

MR. L. : " *You have there a youth of undiscovered modesty and incandescent appearance; his manners are aggressive, his fluency phenomenal; he is a champion spinner of pig-tails for other people.   He is thinking of indentured labourers in the New Hebrides with nothing to brighten their lives but the interest of selecting which of their fellow-sufferers they shall eat next.*"

THE POLITICAL POTBOY

Mr. Winston Churchill, in his remarkable speech at Edinburgh, attacked what he termed the " Pothouse Press ", but himself made use of personalities and abuse hardly becoming in a Minister of the Crown. Mr. Austen Chamberlain was referred to as having " donned an orchid regardless of expense and screwed an eyeglass into his eye regardless of discomfort ".

WINSTON IN UGANDA

Mr. Winston Churchill intends to visit East Africa and Uganda during the recess. He will probably find some interesting and familiar features there.

In 1907 Churchill toured Uganda, and the story of this is told in *My African Journey*.

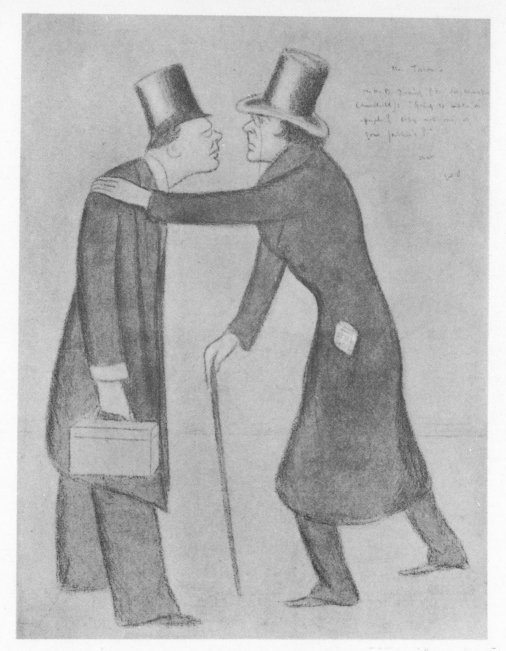

THE TORCH

MR. H. B. IRVING (to Mr. Winston Churchill) : " *Going to make a speech? Why not one of your father's ?* "

At the time of this Max Beerbohm caricature many people still believed that Winston was only a shade of his famous father. The caricature was later printed in Beerhohm's *Fifty Caricatures* (Heinemann, 1913).

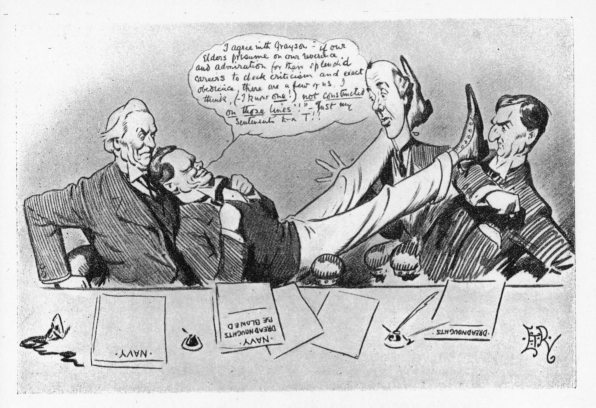

" JUDGING CHARACTER BY CORRESPONDENCE " : OR, THE WINSTON TOUCH

Our artist has curiously few opportunities of attending Cabinet Councils, but, after a careful study of Mr. Winston Churchill's letter to his constituents about the " 8 " (Dreadnoughts) question, in which he light-heartedly casti- gates every axiom and argument of his dear colleagues, he feels sure that the above can be no inaccurate representation of what usually occurs when the Cabinet meets in council.

In 1908 Asquith succeeded Campbell-Bannerman as Prime Minister, and Winston Churchill, aged thirty-four, entered the Cabinet as President of the Board of Trade. Lloyd George became Chancellor of the Exchequer, and both he and Churchill strenuously opposed the Conservative demand for the building of dreadnoughts to be used in the expected war with Germany. However, the Conservatives' cry " We want eight, and we won't wait " gained such public support that their own colleague, Reginald McKenna, First Lord of the Admiralty, threatened to resign unless he got the ships. He won the day, and the building of the dreadnoughts began.

STUDENTS ON THE MAKE

Mr. F. E. Smith : " *Master of epigram—like me !* "
Mr. Winston Churchill : " *Wrote a novel in his youth—like me !* "
Together : " *Travelled in the East—like us. How does it end ?* "

(*Mr. W. F. Monypenny's official Life of Disraeli has just been published.*)

Churchill met F. E. Smith, who became Earl of Birkenhead, in 1906, and years later he wrote : " From that hour our friendship was perfect." Sir Winston's only novel, *Savrola*, was published in 1899.

A BIT OVER THE BORDER

MR. WINSTON CHURCHILL : " *O, you'll tak' the High Road,*
                        An' I'll tak' the Low Road,
                        An' I'll be in Scotland afore ye."

After being M.P. for Oldham, Churchill became Liberal Member for
North-West Manchester in 1906, but was defeated in a by-election in 1908.
He was invited to stand for Dundee, and won with a large majority.
During his election campaign he met Miss Clementine Hozier, and they
were married the same year. In 1910, at the General Election, he retained
his seat at Dundee and became Home Secretary in the new Government.

THE SUCCESSION

MR. CHURCHILL : " *Come, suppose we toss for it, Davey.*"
MR. LLOYD GEORGE : " *Ah, but, Winsie, would either of us as loser abide by the result ?* "

At this time Lloyd George and Winston Churchill were close friends but rivals for the Premiership should Asquith resign.

SOME INOFFENSIVE FANCY COSTUMES

(At a fancy dress ball given recently by two prominent Unionists, complaint was made of Mr. Waldorf Astor, M.P., appearing as a comic peer. Our cartoonist suggests a few fancy costumes which might be worn without the slightest risk of giving offence to anyone.)

MR. WINSTON CHURCHILL AS " A PRETTY GOOD JUDGE".

During his period of office as Home Secretary he was very interested in Prison Reform and did much to better conditions in prisons.

PUNCH   30th August 1911

AN ARTISTIC EFFORT GONE WRONG

As the Labour Party have attempted to paint Mr. Winston Churchill—half-tyrant, half-Caliban.

The impression left on the minds of fair-minded people—a champion of the rights of the country at large.

At this time, although he was still reviled by the Conservatives for what they called his revolutionary ideas, he began to deviate a little from the Radical and Isolationist line he had adopted, and several of his actions as Home Secretary were resented by Left and Labour circles.

C

A CHOICE OF CHARACTERS

OUR ONE AND ONLY WINSTON : " *Let's see, now; shall I go as Demosthenes, d'Artagnan, Dan O'Connell-Leno, or merely the usual Daniel in the lions' den ? The last, I think; and, for all I care, let 'em choose their own den.*"

In 1911 Churchill became First Lord of the Admiralty, and by then he was fully conscious of the German menace to world peace. He was also conscious of being a man of many parts and was quite used to being attacked by the Lion of Public Opinion.

THE HARP THAT ONCE AGAIN

Mr. Winston Churchill moved the Second Reading of the Home Rule Bill yesterday afternoon.

The Asquith Government depended on the votes of the 84 Irish Nationalist Members of Parliament for its majority, and it pledged itself to introduce a Home Rule Bill. Ulster was against the Bill, saying Home Rule meant " Rome Rule ", but Churchill supported it, and he made a daring speech on its behalf in Belfast.

WELL-EARNED INCREMENT

(DESIGN FOR AN ADMIRALTY CHRISTMAS CARD)

The First Lord of the Admiralty was so interested in building up the strength of the Navy that he forgot party politics and became, as Lloyd George complained, absorbed in boilers. New guns and the change-over to oil entailed enormous expense, but in his improvements Winston did not forget the welfare of " Jolly Jack Tar ", and his Naval Estimates of this period were the highest in British history.

UNDER HIS MASTER'S EYE

Scene—Mediterranean, on board the Admiralty yacht, " Enchantress".

Mr. Winston Churchill : " *Any home news ?* "
Mr. Asquith : " *How can there be with you here ?* "

In the two years and nine months before the start of the 1914-18 war the
First Lord spent eight months afloat in the *Enchantress* and visited every
important ship, learning all he could about his " trade ".

CHRISTMAS SHOPPING

MRS. COCOA PRESS : "*Come away from that window, you naughty boy. You have too many of those toys already.*"

Churchill's Naval Estimates at the end of 1913 were over £50,000,000. The Cabinet gasped, Lloyd George threatened to resign, and certain sections of the Press raised a clamour against any extra expenditure.

A SEA-CHANGE

TORY CHORUS (to Winston) : " *You made me love you ; I didn't want to do it.*"

The Conservatives did not like the Naval expenditure any more than the Liberals did, but in the face of German aggression they were forced to comply.
" You Made Me Love You " was a popular song hit by James V. Monaco and Joe McCarthy.

AND HE GETS IT

OLIVER TWIST (A New Version)

JOHN BULL : *I thought I had given you plenty, but if you really want more I suppose you must have it.*

The First Lord threatened to resign and allowed a rumour to spread that he would rejoin the Conservative Party. The Liberals became frightened and, after Winston had knocked a million pounds off his Naval Estimates, they let the Bill pass.

WHY CARSON IS NOT ARRESTED—A GUESS

CHURCHILL (to brother in armaments) : " *Arrest* you, *my dear Carson ?*
What madness ! We've too much respect for the gun trade for that."

Sir Edward Carson, a former Conservative Minister, was the leader of the
Northern Irish who opposed the Home Rule Bill. In the summer of 1913
he started the " Ulster Volunteers ", and this army grew to 100,000 men
by the end of the year. Gun running took place, and rifles and ammunition
were supplied by Germany. Although Winston Churchill was on the
opposing side, his friend F. E. Smith was a supporter of Ulster and
Carson's right-hand man. Labour circles took the opportunity given by
this situation to jibe at Churchill.

A YAWNING CHASM

" The First Lord, who almost immediately afterwards took his seat on the Treasury bench, began to retaliate on Lord Charles by yawning at him."
—Extract from yesterday's Parliamentary report.

Lord Charles Beresford was Commander-in-Chief of the Channel, or principal, Fleet.

LET THE RED BLOOD FLOW

Fe, Fi, Fo, Fum !
I smell the blood of an Ulsterman.
Be he alive or be he dead,
I'll grind his bones for Devlin's bread.

In March 1914, Asquith forced the Irish Nationalist M.P.s to agree to a plan enabling Ulster to vote itself out of the Home Rule Bill. Foreseeing Civil War and bloodshed in Ireland, Churchill made plans for the British Army to occupy all munition dumps, arsenals and strategic positions in Ulster. This scheme was intended to protect Army stores in case Civil War broke out at the same time as the expected war with Germany, but although Asquith announced that a military campaign against Ulster was never intended, Ulstermen persisted then, and for a long time after, in regarding Winston Churchill as a " bloodthirsty ogre ".

TURNING THE TABLES

(*It is announced that Mr. Winston Churchill is spending Easter in Madrid.*)

BONAR AND HIS BOGIES

(The absurd attempt of the Tories to humbug the public by concocting a ridiculous charge against the Government of deliberately plotting a wholesale massacre of Ulsterites, has been completely exposed by the evidence laid before Parliament during the past week.)

JOHNNY BULL : *" Take them away, Bonar.   You can't curdle my blood with those silly things ! They've had all the stuffing knocked out of them ! "*

Bonar Law, the Conservative leader, never lost an opportunity to try to vilify the Prime Minister and the First Lord of the Admiralty.

EVENING NEWS
30th November 1914

THE VICTORY CHORUS

Three quite confident speeches about the war situation were given on successive days by three ministers, Churchill, Kitchener and Lloyd George. This cartoon was published on Winston Churchill's fortieth birthday — an interesting " half way house " in his career.

CHURCHILL S'EN VA-T-EN GUERRE

WINSTON (through force of nautical habit) to SIR JOHN FRENCH : " *Come aboard, sir !* "

After the failure of the Dardanelles campaign, public opinion turned against Churchill, and when a Coalition Government was formed the Conservatives insisted that he relinquish office as First Lord of the Admiralty. Asquith offered him the minor post of Chancellor of the Duchy of Lancaster, and he accepted because he could still remain a member of the War Council. However, he was not included in the War Committee which replaced the War Council, and he decided to stay no longer in " well-paid inactivity ". In Nov. 1915 Major Churchill of the Oxfordshire Yeomanry landed in France at Sir John French's headquarters.

WINSTON (sheathing his Sunday-paper weapon in his best Blenheim manner): "*After all, some say 'The pen is mightier than the sword.'*"

There was strong opposition when the Conservatives heard that Sir John French intended to give Major Churchill command of a brigade, and Asquith was forced to tell French that he could have only a battalion. Lieutenant-Colonel Churchill of the Sixth Royal Scots Fusiliers was popular with the troops, but he pined for the excitement of Parliament, and in the summer of 1916 he resigned his commission. Back in the House of Commons, but without office, he turned his immense energy to journalism as a means of helping to win the war.

PUNCH   13th June 1917

MR. WINSTON CHURCHILL (with eye on the Air Board): "*Any uniform suits me, thank you.*"

In December 1916 the Asquith Government fell, and Lloyd George became Prime Minister. He wished to give Winston Churchill office in his new Government, but Bonar Law objected. At last, however, in July 1917, Lloyd George was able to offer Churchill a choice between the Air Ministry and the Ministry of Munitions. He chose the latter. It did not mean a seat in the Cabinet but, as he had been out of office for twenty months, it was the end of political exile.

MR. G. N. BARNES SITS ON THE WINSTON VOLCANO

Mr. Barnes made a speech in Glasgow, criticizing Churchill and the Dardanelles. He described the Government as " living on the top of a veritable volcano", but this, as *Punch* pointed out, could have " no reference to the Minister of Munitions, who, as everybody knows, cannot be sat upon".

PORTRAIT OF WINSTON BY MR. MOSLEY
A PROMISING YOUNG ARTIST

After winning the " Coupon " Election of December 1918, Lloyd George made Winston Churchill Secretary of State for War, with the Air Ministry amalgamated under him. While he was in Paris at the Peace Conference there was a debate in Parliament on the Aerial Navigation Bill, and Mr. Mosley, aged twenty-two, attacked the War Minister as being lacking in imagination in aviation matters. *Punch* was amused at the idea of anyone considering Winston to be a doddering old fossil at the age of forty-four.

" STRAWS " SHOW WHICH WAY THE WIND BLOWS

Lloyd George's Coalition Government was defeated in several by-elections.

PUNCH   27th August 1919

MR. WINSTON CHURCHILL (returning from the Rhine) : " *What ! No official motor-car ? Well, this brings the Peace home to one.*"

That summer the Secretary of State for War toured the Rhineland to inspect the Army of Occupation.

D

DAILY EXPRESS 8th September 1919

"WE DON'T KNOW WHERE WE'RE GOING, BUT WE'RE ON OUR WAY."

The Civil War in Russia was at its height, and in 1918 Britain had sent troops to Archangel, the Caucasus and Siberia to protect oil interests and to keep Allied materials from falling into the hands of the Bolsheviks. Eventually British forces were withdrawn, but since the Government continued to send ammunition and war materials to the White Russian armies the general public did not know whether they were officially at war or not.

PUBLIC : " *You did it on me with your Sidney Street-Antwerp-Gallipoli 'fluence, but not in this stunt !* "

The Secretary of State for War was anti-Bolshevik, referring in one speech to " the foul baboonery of Bolshevism ", and the British public viewed the situation with alarm, feeling that there should be non-intervention and that the Russians should be allowed to settle their own affairs.

"O WAD SOME POWER THE GIFTIE GIE US
TO SEE OURSELS AS ITHERS SEE US!"

WINSTON : " *You couldn't wear a hat like this. It would make you look
so silly!* "

Churchill's fondness for odd hats has always been a favourite subject
for cartoonists. At this period the Labour Party was furious because he
still favoured intervention in Russia, and he was attacked by Labour
leaders.

WINSTON'S BAG

HE HUNTS LIONS AND BRINGS HOME DECAYED CATS

The War Minister was preparing to send British arms to help Poland's attack on Russia, and the man-in-the-street became worried in case there would be another Gallipoli.

CHIEF EAR-TO-THE-GROUND WINSTON

The Polish attack on Russia failed, Russia invaded Poland, and for a few weeks it looked as though a major European war might break out again.

" THE CROCK "—OFFICIAL

DOCTOR : " *I tell you you are C.3, and who ever heard of me making a mistake ?* "

Churchill had lost much of the Radicalism of his youth and was veering again towards the Conservatives. He had no use for the Labour Party.

MR. CHURCHILL SEES RED

Army uniform (1) as it is ; (2) as it was before the war and will be again ; and (3) as, to suit Mr. Churchill's Marlborough traditions, it should have been.

There was a rumour that the Government intended to spend three millions on new uniforms for the army, replacing khaki with the traditional scarlet.

WINSTONSKY

HORRIFYING EFFECT OF CONCENTRATION ON RUSSIAN AFFAIRS

(" *Lenin I believe is an aristocrat, and Trotsky is a journalist. My right hon. friend the Secretary for War is an embodiment of both.*"—*Mr. Lloyd George.*)

Although Soviet authority took control in Russia in the spring of 1920, Winston Churchill continued to be anti-Bolshevik.

THE WELLS OF TRUTH

H. G. Wells was in favour of the Russian experiment and he was an admirer of Lenin. Articles which he wrote for the *Sunday Express* were later published in a book, *Russia in the Shadows*.

" KEEP THE HATE-FIRES BURNING. "

Ivor Novello's " Keep the Home-fires Burning " was one of the most
popular songs of the 1914-18 war.
The Labour Party accused Winston Churchill of obstructing the newly-
formed League of Nations with his views on Soviet Russia.

A LITTLE BIT ON THE TOP

WINSOME WINNIE : " *Isn't it a perfect dream !* "

British troops stationed in Mesopotamia to preserve order were costing
£40,000,000 a year, and Winston Churchill, no longer having the Bolshevik
bogey to take up his attention, was asked to turn his restless energy towards
the Middle East and see if he could save some money for the taxpayer.

A NEW HAT

In January 1921 Churchill left the War Office and became Secretary of State for the Colonies.

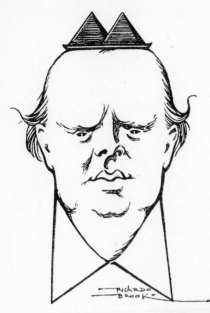

IT IS SURMISED THAT THE RESULT OF MR. CHURCHILL'S
ART STUDY AMONG THE PYRAMIDS IS SURE TO BE FELT

The Colonial Secretary held a conference in Cairo to discuss
the situation in the Middle East. An uprising had been
suppressed in Mesopotamia, and the Arabs were seething
because the French, who had been given the Mandate of
Syria by the Peace Conference, had thrown out the Emir
Feisal. Lawrence of Arabia was the Colonial Secretary's chief
adviser at this conference, and between them they drew up a
plan for a peaceful settlement in Mesopotamia, Transjordan
and Palestine. While in Egypt, Winston visited the Pyramids
and devoted his few hours of leisure to painting.

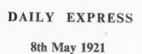

DAILY EXPRESS

8th May 1921

THE CHURCHILL-WELLS CONTROVERSY

CHURCHILL : " *You were only fourteen days in Russia !* "
WELLS : " *Your mother's an American !* "

H. G. Wells visited Russia in September 1920 and returned anti-Marxist,
although still an admirer of Lenin. Winston Churchill's mother, Jeanette
Jerome, was the daughter of a New York business man who at one time
owned and edited the *New York Times*.

BRINGING HIS WARES TO MARKET

IN THE HOUSE OF COMMONS YESTERDAY MR. WINSTON CHURCHILL MADE HIS STATEMENT ON THE MIDDLE EAST

The Cabinet accepted the Colonial Secretary's plan for the Middle East. Among other things, troops were withdrawn from Iraq, and order was maintained by the Air Force instead of the Army, a procedure which cut the cost from thirty millions to five millions a year. The Arab world was satisfied, and eleven years later when Lawrence of Arabia sent Churchill a copy of his *Seven Pillars of Wisdom*, it was inscribed : " Winston Churchill who made a happy ending to this show . . . after we set our hands to making an honest settlement, all our work still stands : the countries have gone forward, our interests have been saved, and nobody killed, either on one side or the other."

REYNOLDS'S NEWSPAPER

17th July 1921

WINSTON

MR. CHURCHILL SURVEYS THE WORLD FROM CHINA TO PERU

As Colonial Secretary, Winston Churchill had to keep careful watch on a wide horizon.

JOHN : " *Just look what your dog ' Mespot ' has done !* "
WINSTON : " *You'll pardon me, sir, my dog's name is ' Irak '.* "

(*The Government seems to be trying to evade responsibility for Mesopotamia by calling it Irak.*)

Part of the Middle East settlement was the establishment of the Emir Feisal as King of Mesopotamia, which was rechristened Iraq.

DISARMAMENT AND THE MAN

MR. WINSTON CHURCHILL (late Minister of War by Land and Sea):
"*Of course my true genius is bellicose ; but if they insist on my representing
my country at the Washington Conference I must make the sacrifice.*"

A Disarmament Conference was held in Washington in the autumn
of 1921, but the Colonial Secretary did not attend.

E

The Rt. Hon. Winston Churchill.

HATS off to "Pinnace." It is no TERMINOLOGICAL INEXACTITUDE to say that they MINISTER most capably to smokers of taste. "Pinnace" make troubles FLY and PILOT you to satisfaction. They are equally popular with NAVY, ARMY, AIR FORCE, COLONIES, HOME and TRADE, that's a fact you can't ESCAPE from.

'Pinnace'

The " Quality " Navy Cut

Cigarettes

"Pinnace" are the finest quality Virginia Cigarettes made. More than value, irrespective of the real photo, given with them. These are given as an advertisement and in no way detract from the super-excellent quality of the Cigarette.

Two Thousand Pounds
Football Money Prizes

Full particulars of competitions in each packet. Over 1,000 cash prizes to be won. In exchange for 25 small photos a cabinet photo of one of over 1,000 footballers *free*. Albums for small photos, 1s., post free 1s. 3d.

10 for 6d.   20 for 11½d.   50 for 2/5

GODFREY PHILLIPS, LIMITED, LONDON

Winston Churchill took up painting in the summer of 1915, after he left the Admiralty. He experimented first with a box of water-colours belonging to his children, but soon turned to oils and found great solace in splashing bold, vivid colours on canvas. In 1921 he exhibited five landscapes in Paris under the name of Charles Morin, and four were sold for £30 each.

TAKING THE CAKE

NO MATTER WHAT SORT OF CAKE YOU MAKE,
OR HOW MUCH CARE AND PAINS YOU TAKE,
OR RICH OR PLAIN DOESN'T MATTER A BIT,
SOMEBODY'LL TURN UP THEIR NOSE AT IT

An International Economic Conference was held at Genoa in 1922.

LOW'S ZOO.   VI.—THE WINSTONOCEROS AND PREY

(*This interesting pachyderm has the appearance of being armourplated, but is sensitive to tickling at the joints of the harness. Reports of its savage nature are probably exaggerated, but it has been known to destroy imaginary enemies with great fury.*)

This is the mental picture most British Socialists had of Winston Churchill at this period, and it persisted for many years.

AT THE IRISH DERBY

CHURCHILL (the Trainer) : " *Hang it all, Collins ; she'll never do like this !*
She's got her legs crossed again ! "

The Colonial Secretary was a member of the Cabinet Committee dealing
with the problem of Ireland. Fighting between the Sinn Fein Party and
the British " Black and Tans " was fierce, and when Michael Collins
and Arthur Griffiths came to London to sign the Treaty, which gave
Ireland Dominion status, Winston Churchill worked tirelessly to help
them establish a Provisional Government.

LOST IN DUNDEE

In November 1922 Winston Churchill was defeated at Dundee in the General Election, and for the first time since 1900 he was out of Parliament.

MR. CHURCHILL AND FRIEND

WINSTON : *" We have both made history and we have both written it.
Let us exchange headgear."*

While in the South of France recuperating from an operation for appendi-
citis, Churchill finished writing the first volume of *The World Crisis*,
which appeared in April 1923.

IT IS RUMOURED THAT SOME INTERESTING ADDITIONS ARE TO BE MADE TO
THE FAUNA OF EPPING FOREST

After being out of Parliament for two years, Winston Churchill, who had
by this time severed his connection with the Liberals, stood as a " Con-
stitutionalist " with Conservative support at the " Red Letter " Election
of 1924. He contested Epping and won the seat.

A PRELIMINARY CANTER

In a pre-election speech at Edinburgh Churchill attacked Socialism,
which was then under the leadership of Ramsay MacDonald.

THE RECRUITING PARADE

The original drawing is in Sir Winston's possession.

THE NEW BRITANNIA

("*Let Britannia*," concluded *Mr. Churchill*, "*cast off the ridiculous and dishonourable disguise and rags made in Germany and in Russia with which the Socialists seek to drape her. Let her reveal herself once again, sedate, majestic on her throne.*") (*Loud Cheers*)

A few days after the General Election, Stanley Baldwin, the Conservative Prime Minister, made Churchill the Chancellor of the Exchequer.

THE SULTAN CHOOSES HIS FAVOURITE

Winston's new appointment astonished many people, including Austen Chamberlain, the new Foreign Secretary, and was a cause of grief to others, one of whom, Sir Robert Horne, was a former Chancellor.

DAILY MAIL

8th November 1924

THE TOPPER

NOW, THAT'S SOMETHING LIKE A HAT!

Although many Conservatives still disliked Winston Churchill for his political past, Stanley Baldwin was anxious to please him.

THERE ARE GIANTS IN THESE DAYS

Speaking at the Guildhall Banquet in London, Stanley Baldwin likened
Austen Chamberlain and Winston Churchill to the guardian giants of the
City.

NOW COMES THE TUG-OF-WAR

HOLD THEM, WINSTON !

In the face of increasing expenditure, the suspicion of the general public, the disapproval of some Tories, and the whole-hearted opposition of the Socialists, the new Chancellor of the Exchequer had a difficult time.

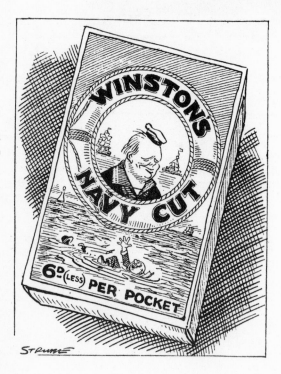

DAILY EXPRESS

13th February 1925

(*with apologies to John Player & Sons*)

There was speculation as to whether the price of tobacco would rise in the coming Budget. Cigarettes were elevenpence for twenty at this time.

THE DANGER SIGN

IT HAS BEEN DECIDED TO ADOPT NO UNIONIST CANDIDATE FOR THE OLDHAM BY-ELECTION

When Churchill presented his first Budget, Philip Snowden, the Labour ex-Chancellor, jeered at the Protectionist tax on artificial silk, accusing the new Chancellor of having changed his views about taxing silk imports. "There is nothing wrong with change if it is in the right direction," replied Churchill. "To improve is to change. To be perfect is to change often."

—BUT FELIX KEEPS ON WALKING

In 1925 the British coal-mining industry was in such a bad state that the
Government subsidized the miners while a Commission made an inves-
tigation. This, of course, was hard on the tax-payer. Felix the Cat was
a popular film-cartoon character of the twenties, and the subject of a song
hit.

POOR DADDY!

THE POSITION OF PARENTS SEEKING ACCOMMODATION WITH CHILDREN IS
OFTEN POSITIVELY HEARTRENDING

The Civil Service did not take kindly to the Chancellor's economy
campaign.

F

THE " STEP " BROTHER

MR. CHURCHILL SAYS HE HAS LONG BEEN CONSIDERING THE WHOLE QUESTION
OF THE ROAD FUND AND ITS " RELATIONSHIP " TO THE EXCHEQUER

The Road Fund was established in 1920, and into it was paid " hypo-
theticated revenue " from motor spirit and motor tax. In 1926 it was
decided that a third of this revenue should be treated as sumptuary
taxation.

MR. BALDWIN ON HIMSELF

(" *The life of a shop girl and that of a Prime Minister are very similar. . . . The only difference is that she has to give people what they want ; I have to say that they can't have it.*")

PUNCH **24th March 1926**

THE OLD FOX : " *What a shocking sight ! I wonder who taught that wicked young cub to rob henroosts ?*"

On 17th March 1926, Lloyd George made a speech in the House attacking the " raiding propensities " of the Chancellor of the Exchequer. Lloyd George himself instituted Unemployment Insurance and Health Benefits.

THE KING OF CLUBS!

The public regarded another of the Chancellor's Budgets with gloom.

Winston

This cartoon was published in Low's *Lions and Lambs* (Cape, 1928) and was used as a front-cover for Philip Guedalla's *Mr. Churchill* when it was reprinted by Pan Books.

CHURCHILL BLOCKS THE WAY

The Coal Commission issued its report on 11th March 1926, but neither Baldwin, the miners, nor the Trade Unions would accept it. It was felt that the Treasury stood in the way of settlement, and when wage cuts were introduced a coal stoppage started on 30th April. The result was the General Strike.

THE OBLIGING CHANCELLOR

(MR. CHURCHILL PROMISED THE MINERS THAT IF THEY WOULD WRITE A
LETTER AGREEING TO CONCESSIONS HE WOULD SEE THEM THROUGH)

BALDWIN´: *I am sorry to hear you are going to resign !*
CHURCHILL : *I don't think ! I promised not to leave you until the last
moment of your official existence ; but then——*

The coal strike continued for a long time after the General Strike had
collapsed.

THE CHINA EGG

WINSTON : " *Who put this Egg in while I was away ?* "

The Chancellor returned from a holiday in Rome, where he met Mussolini and studied the Facist régime, to find there was a crisis in China. The Chinese Civil War had been raging for some time, and British interests at Shanghai and elsewhere being threatened, Britain started negotiations with the Cantonese Government about a revision of the trade treaty. When these fell through and there was rioting in Hankow, Britain despatched troops to Shanghai to maintain order.

THE RIDDLE OF THE SPHINX

As usual, the Public in the person of Strube's Little Man wondered what secrets the Chancellor of the Exchequer's Budget would disclose.

BRINGING GRIST TO THE MILL

THE NAVAL ESTIMATES SHOW A SAVING OF ONLY £100,000 !

HIS SURPLUS—FOURS

During Baldwin's administration Britain was forced back on to the gold standard, and this was followed by deflation and mass unemployment.

Baggy suits of plus-fours were extremely popular with men at this period.

A DEFIANT TEAM

In 1927 Stanley Baldwin undertook that none of his Ministers would write for the Press, but both Lord Birkenhead and Winston Churchill were busy contributing articles to the magazines of William Randolph Hearst, the American newspaper owner.

EXPELLED FROM HIS TRADE UNION, WINSTON WATCHES REAL BRICKLAYERS
DOING THE JOB THOROUGHLY, AND WONDERS HOW SOON IT WILL BE BEFORE
ALL HIS PALS ARE ON THE DOLE

At his country home, Chartwell, in Kent, the Chancellor of the Exchequer
built a cottage on the estate, working with a professional bricklayer until
he could lay a brick a minute. In 1928 he was invited by Mr. Hicks, the
General Secretary, to join the Amalgamated Union of Building Trade
Workers, paid a fee of five shillings, and was rated as an "adult
apprentice". The T.U.C. made an outcry, denouncing his act as "a
painful insult to members of the union". But he kept his membership
ticket.

THE AMATEUR BRICKLAYER : " *There, that doesn't look so bad, and perhaps people won't notice that I've pinched the mortar.*"

(*Mr. Churchill has been bricklaying and Budget-making in the holidays. Philip Snowden points out that his so-called surplus has been made by raiding the Sinking Fund.*)

Despite the T.U.C.'s refusal to welcome him in the Bricklayers' Union, Winston Churchill built a large part of two cottages and a swimming pool at Chartwell with his own hands during the next twelve years.

HOIST WITH THEIR OWN PETARD

(The Opposition's attack on the Government in connection with Lord Lloyd's resignation proved a great fiasco, Mr. Churchill in particular being severely handled by both Mr. Arthur Henderson and Mr. Ramsay MacDonald.)

PUNCH   12th March 1930

PHIL AND WIN, THE FAMOUS BACK-CHAT COMEDIANS

EVERY-OTHER-DAILY PERFORMANCE

Philip Snowden was Chancellor of the Exchequer in the Labour Government and, as a former Chancellor, Winston Churchill often criticized his successor. This gave cause for many acrimonious verbal exchanges.

TELLING THE WORLD

THE NINETEEN-YEAR-OLD SON OF MR. WINSTON CHURCHILL IS TELLING
THE CHIEF CITIES OF THE UNITED STATES ALL ABOUT OUR HOME POLITICS.
THE ABOVE IS AN EXTRACT FROM ONE OF HIS SPEECHES

MEDITATIONS OF AN EX-CHANCELLOR

Lord Irwin (now Lord Halifax), Viceroy of India at this time, was in favour of granting India her freedom.   Stanley Baldwin supported this policy, but Winston Churchill opposed it, and speaking to a huge meeting in the Albert Hall on 18th March 1931, he said : " I am against this surrender to Gandhi.   I am against these conversations and agreements between Lord Irwin and Mr. Gandhi."

RAMSAY MACBETH

LADY WINSTON MACBETH : "*Infirm of purpose ! Give ME the daggers !*"
(*Macbeth II, ii.*)

In 1931 Ramsay MacDonald formed a National Government with himself as Prime Minister. Conservative members were in the majority, and
Stanley Baldwin was the power behind the throne. Winston Churchill
was not offered a post in this Government ; he and MacDonald were
old antagonists, and since he had resigned from Baldwin's " Shadow
Cabinet " in 1930 " Honest Stan " was no longer his friend.

Sir Winston has the original drawing of this cartoon.

" YAH, UNTOUCHABLE ! "

Churchill joined the die-hards of the Tory Party in consistently opposing
Stanley Baldwin's policy of granting Dominion status to India.

THE WOOD-CARVINGS OF M'BONGO M'BONGO

No. V.—A Streuthsayer
or Prophet of Doom

Winston Churchill realized the dangers of the Nazi menace as far back as 1932 but Parliament and the public refused to listen to his repeated warnings.

PUNCH   29th July 1936

THE MANIKIN AND THE SUPER-MAN ; or, "IF I WERE DOING IT"

(*After an engraving entitled "Malbrook" in the Bibliothèque Nationale, Paris.*)

SIR THOMAS INSKIP AND MR. WINSTON CHURCHILL

In the Defence debate in the Commons, Churchill attacked Sir Thomas Inskip and the Government for complacency and begged Parliament not to forget Germany's ruthless rearmament, and to act accordingly.

A FAMILY VISIT

"IT WAS A GREAT WORK, AND I WISH YOU COULD NOW ADD ANOTHER
CHAPTER TO YOUR OWN CAREER."

During the years he was not in office, Sir Winston devoted much of his
energy to writing his monumental *Life of Marlborough*.

TRIBUNE 13th January 1939

A SQUARE DEAL IS WHAT
THE RAILWAYS SAY THEY HAVE NOT,
BUT A BLOCK OF WOOD GRACES
MANY SHOULDERS IN HIGH PLACES.

CIVIL & MILITARY GAZETTE, LAHORE 30th June 1939

WINSTON'S WARNING.
"JULY, AUGUST AND SEPTEMBER MUST BE CONSIDERED AS THE MONTHS IN WHICH THE TENSION IN EUROPE WILL BECOME MOST SEVERE."

YOU'RE TELLING ME!

The world still persisted in giving this American slang rejoinder to Winston Churchill's repeated warnings against Nazi aggression.

THE OLD SEA-DOG

"ANY TELEGRAM FOR ME ?"

War with Germany seemed inevitable, but although the Press and public clamoured for Winston Churchill to be taken into the Government, Neville Chamberlain still did not offer him office. Like Drake, playing bowls before the arrival of the Spanish Armada, Churchill was forced to wait.

" ALL IS FORGIVEN : WELCOME HOME "

When war started Neville Chamberlain was forced to invite Winston
Churchill, Anthony Eden and Duff Cooper to rejoin the Conservative
Government, Churchill becoming again First Lord of the Admiralty,
the position he had held at the commencement of the 1914-18 war.

BRITISH LION AND GALLIC COCK

" YOU JUMP THROUGH THE HOOP FIRST, DEAR COCK, I SHALL FOLLOW
AFTER ! "

A German attempt to disrupt Allied unity by suggesting that French
soldiers, manning the Maginot Line, were being sent first into battle.

"BUT YOU SHOULDA SEEN THE ONE THAT GOT AWAY!"

The great German liner *Bremen*, which had been sheltering in Murmansk, was allowed to reach Germany, being spared by the British submarine *Salmon*, which rigidly observed the conventions of International Law.

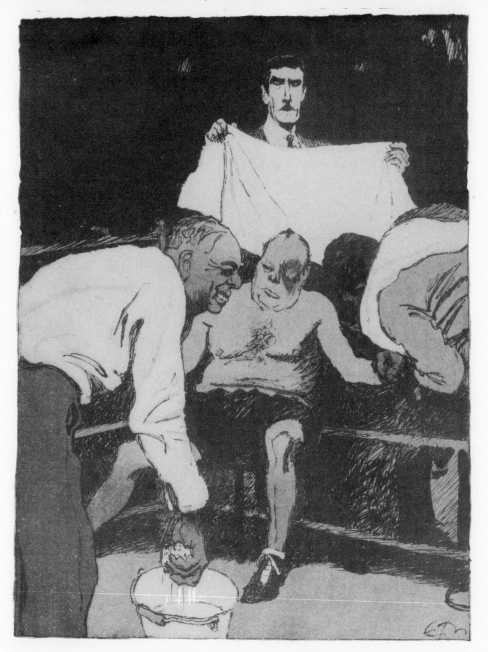

AFTER THE FIRST ROUND

CHURCHILL RECEIVED SEVERAL HARD BODY-BLOWS.   UNDOUBTEDLY WE
HAVE WON THE FIRST ROUND !

Leslie Hore-Belisha, Secretary of State for War, is acting as one of
Churchill's seconds.

CHURCHILL DIVIDES GERMANY

"NOW, DEAR CHILDREN, WHICH PIECE SHALL I CUT FOR EACH OF YOU?"

" CIGAR-IN-THE-FACE 'WIN' "

U-boats, according to Mr. Winston Churchill, are being destroyed at a rate far superior to that at which Germany can replace them.

This cartoon was reprinted in the *Daily Telegraph* on 27th January 1940.

VOELKISCHER BEOBACHTER

BERLIN   January 1940

THE   GERMAN   COUNTER-BLOCKADE

JOHN BULL : *Damn!   Once again less tonnage!*

German newspapers reported that they had sunk many British ships.

This Dutch cartoon was reprinted in the *Daily Express* on 31st January 1940. It was the 151st day of the war, and the little neutrals were faced with extinction if Hitler won. Churchill is shown urging them to drop neutrality in favour of co-operation with the Allies.

CARELESS TALK MAY BETRAY VITAL SECRETS

" HUSH, MY DEAR ! YOU NEVER KNOW WHO'S LISTENING ! "

Ministry of Information posters about " Careless Talk " were displayed everywhere.

CHURCHILL, THE BRAGGART

THE RULER OF ALL THE SEAS
WEEPS MANY A BITTER TEAR.
THE POOR MAN CAN HARDLY GRASP IT,
THAT THIS IS THE END TO THE DREAM OF " THE SUPREMACY
   OF THE SEAS"

KLADDERADATSCH,   BERLIN   February 1940

" BUT NEVILLE, WHAT ARE YOU DOING ? "
" I'M TRAINING FOR MY NEXT JOURNEY TO FRANCE."

Evidently the Germans were sure that Mr. Chamberlain
would have to swim the Channel.

AFTER THE RUSSO-FINNISH ARMISTICE

" CHURCHILL, IF YOUR POLICY MAKES YOU SUFFER ANOTHER DEFEAT LIKE
THIS, I SHALL DEPRIVE YOUR FIRM OF THE TITLE OF COURT SUPPLIERS ! "

During the first seven months of war the biggest death roll was on the
Russo-Finnish battlefield.

H

A TOTALITARIAN ECLIPSE HAS BEEN ARRANGED

On 4th April a statement was issued from 10 Downing Street that the
First Lord of the Admiralty, as the Senior Service Minister, would
preside over the Military Co-ordination Committee. This gave the Press
and public fresh confidence.

THE NEW BRITISH BOXING TEAM

IT IS REPORTED THAT A WAR CABINET IS BEING FORMED

The Allies were being driven back in Europe. Neville Chamberlain was preparing to resign, and Churchill was the likeliest Minister to form a new Cabinet.

THE QUESTION OF
NEUTRALITY

MR. CHURCHILL HAS OPENED IT,
BUT GERMANY HAS WITHOUT DOUBT
GIVEN HIM THE PROPER ANSWER.
NOW HE MAY TREMBLE IN FEAR
        OF THE NEXT REPLY

The German expression is
" to cut into a question "

TWO-GUN WINSTON

On 11th May Winston Churchill formed a new Government, with himself
as Prime Minister and Minister of Defence.

Mr. Churchill last night : *"We are ready to face it !"*

The situation of the Allied Forces in France became more desperate in face of the victorious German advance, and the Prime Minister went to Paris to discuss matters with the French Government. On the 18th May General Gamelin said he could guarantee the safety of Paris for only another two days.

The affectionate way in which most Britons regarded the new Prime Minister. The slogan " Go to it—and keep at it " was displayed on many Ministry of Information posters.

THE JULY HANDICAP

The retention of Neville Chamberlain, as Lord President of the Council in the National Coalition Government, was regarded as a severe handicap by many people.

A DROP OF WHAT YOU FANCY . . .

The song " A Little of What You Fancy Does You Good ", was one of Marie Lloyd's great hits.

CHURCHILL SEES SWASTIKAS EVERYWHERE

CHURCHILL : "*Hell! I must have had a drop too much tonight. This cross is really my cross.*"

A FALL OF SHOOTING STARS

CHURCHILL : " *A star falls. If someone has seen it and made a wish, that will be the end of me.*"

Reproduced in *Der Sturmer*.

NATAL DAILY NEWS   August 1940

" WE'LL WAIT ! "

Both Britain and America tried to persuade Mussolini to keep out of the war, but he was determined to avenge himself for Britain's sanctions against Italy in her war with Abyssinia, and on 10th June 1940 he finally declared war and attacked Yugoslavia. Broadcasting that night, President Roosevelt said " the hand that held the dagger has struck it into the back of its neighbour "

MAY THE MANY OWE MUCH TO *THESE* FEW

The Battle of Britain was at its height, depending almost entirely upon its airmen—the First of the Few. The War Cabinet included Mr. C. R. Attlee, the Labour leader, Mr. Arthur Greenwood, Lord Halifax, Lord Beaverbrook, Sir John Anderson, Mr. Ernest Bevin and Sir Kingsley Wood.

THE DEPTH CHARGE

The Prime Minister is personally devoting himself to the problem of beating the U-boat.

"I LIKE THEIR NERVE"

Mr. Wendell Willkie, Roosevelt's opponent in the recent American Presidential Election, paid a visit to Britain.

BRITISH WAR AIMS?

WHY DOES ENGLAND WAGE THIS WAR ?   WHY ?
CHURCHILL DARE NOT MAKE A REPLY.   HE REMAINS DUMB.
WE KNOW QUITE WELL WHY ONE AVOIDS
    TO GIVE A STRAIGHT ANSWER TO THESE QUESTIONS—
WE, HOWEVER, NEED NOT MAKE A SECRET OF THE AIM FOR WHICH WE STRIVE,
WE FIGHT FOR A FREE GERMAN LIFE !

TIME AND TIDE RECALLS . . .

. . . THAT MR. WINSTON CHURCHILL ALWAYS HAD A PERSONALITY TO CONJURE WITH.

This drawing appeared in *Time and Tide* on 8th June 1928 and was reprinted in the issue for 17th May 1941.

DER STURMER, NUREMBERG 4th September 1941

A LITTLE WHILE AGO CHURCHILL AND MISTER ROOSEVELT PLAYED AT CHARADES THEY IMPERSONATED " SIRENS BRINGING HAPPINESS TO ALL THE WORLD ", BY WHICH THEY RIDICULE THEMSELVES

THE JEW HAS ALL THREE IN HIS HAND

Der Sturmer, published by Julius Streicher, was fanatically anti-Jewish. Streicher was tried with the other top-ranking Nazi war criminals at Nuremburg and hanged.

DE MISTHOORN, AMSTERDAM 18th October 1941

CHURCHILL'S LIFE WORK

This cartoon was reproduced in *Der Sturmer*.

NEARING THE SHOW-DOWN

After Germany's initial success in Russia, the tide of victory turned.
Britain sent war supplies through Persia, and the severity of the Russian
winter helped to defeat Hitler's troops.

THE MODERN ICARUS!

In mythical times Icarus and his father Daedalus attempted to fly from Crete to Italy, wearing wings fastened on by wax. Icarus soared so high that the sun melted the wax, and he fell into the sea, giving his name to that part of it.

67 To-day

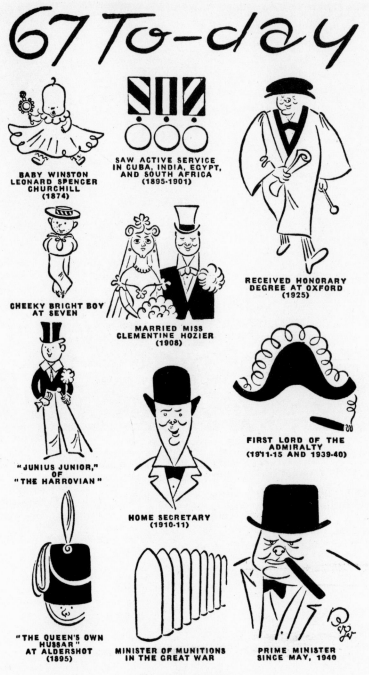

BABY WINSTON LEONARD SPENCER CHURCHILL (1874)

SAW ACTIVE SERVICE IN CUBA, INDIA, EGYPT, AND SOUTH AFRICA (1895-1901)

CHEEKY BRIGHT BOY AT SEVEN

MARRIED MISS CLEMENTINE HOZIER (1908)

RECEIVED HONORARY DEGREE AT OXFORD (1925)

"JUNIUS JUNIOR," OF "THE HARROVIAN"

HOME SECRETARY (1910-11)

FIRST LORD OF THE ADMIRALTY (1911-15 AND 1939-40)

"THE QUEEN'S OWN HUSSAR" AT ALDERSHOT (1895)

MINISTER OF MUNITIONS IN THE GREAT WAR

PRIME MINISTER SINCE MAY, 1940

67 TO-DAY

Mr. Winston Churchill is sixty-seven to-day. Our readers will join with us, we know, in wishing our fighting Prime Minister many happy returns of the day. Here is a " potted " version of his amazing career specially drawn for the NEWS OF THE WORLD *by Oscar Berger, the famous international artist.*

By this time every man and woman in Britain was mobilized.

OVER ON THE BRIGHT SIDE!

The Japanese attacked the Americans at Pearl Harbour on 7th December, and Britain declared war on Japan the following day. But despite this bad news from the Pacific, there were advances on the Russian and Libyan fronts.

ACCENT ON THE WIN

Poy retired in 1938, but occasionally he drew cartoons on special occasions until his death in 1948. The above was drawn for the *Daily Mail*, but was not published. It first appeared in Fieldfare's *The End of a Tale : A Tribute to Poy*.

A HAPPY NEW YEAR

The strength and activities of the R.A.F. were increasing and upon the
signing of the United Nations Pact in Washington plans were drawn up
for even greater strength and co-ordination.

—by Illingworth.

The Prime Minister again visited America to consult with President Roosevelt and the Chiefs of Staff. Upon his return he informed Parliament that there might be impending misfortunes in the war with Japan, and in the face of some hostile attacks from Members and the Press on 27th January he asked for a Vote of Confidence.

. . . BUT THE MELODY LINGERS ON!

The Prime Minister ended his speech on 27th January with the words :
" I stand by my original programme, blood, toil, tears and sweat, which
is all I have ever offered, to which I added, five months later, ' many
shortcomings, mistakes and disappointments '. But it is because I see the
light gleaming behind the clouds and broadening on our path, that I
make so bold now as to demand a declaration of confidence of the House
of Commons as an additional weapon in the armoury of the United
Nations."

WINTERTON'S NIGHTMARE

In a debate in the House of Commons on 21st May 1942 as to whether the war should be controlled by a committee of Chiefs of Staff headed by the Minister of Defence (Churchill) or whether it should be run by one man (Churchill) some Members of Parliament, including Earl Winterton, thought that the latter state existed already.

DRUNKEN " WELTANSCHAUUNG "

**CHURCHILL TRIES TO FIND LUCK IN DRINK,
BUT THE BOTTLE DISTORTS THE VIEW**

" Weltanschauung " means " conception of the world ".

DON'T WORRY HIM, BOYS—HE PROMISED
YOU SHALL GO

During July it was decided to abandon all plans for crossing the Channel
in 1942 ; instead, it was arranged that there would be Anglo-American
landings in French North Africa during the autumn or winter.

THE BULLDOG HAS WINGS

On 12th August 1942, the Prime Minister flew from Cairo to Moscow
to visit Stalin and discuss the question of a Second Front. A British film,
The Lion Has Wings, was shown early in the war.

STILL TRYING TO RIDE 'EM BOTH

A number of critics at this time thought that the Prime Minister should confine his activities to politics and let military experts deal with the carrying on of the war.

TIME AND TIDE 21st November 1942

ANOTHER MIRACLE HARVEST

On 23rd October 1942, the Battle of Alamein was launched, and on 8th November the Anglo-American forces landed in North Africa. The first fruits of victory began to appear.

DAILY MAIL   **30th November 1942**

" IF OUR VOICE WERE EQUAL TO IT, ' A HAPPY BIRTHDAY TO
YOU ' WOULD BE NICE."

The Allied invasion of French North Africa—Operation
Torch—began successfully on November 8th. The Prime
Minister celebrated his sixty-eighth birthday on the 30th.

DAILY EXPRESS   27th January 1943

" WELL, IF IT ISN'T THE WIDOW FATIMA, WHO IS IT ? JUST TELL
ME THAT ! "

The Prime Minister flew to Casablanca for talks with President
Roosevelt, General de Gaulle, General Giraud and others.
The presence of the Prime Minister and the President was a
well-kept secret until a Press Conference on the 24th, at which
de Gaulle and Giraud were forced to shake hands before all the
reporters and photographers. From Casablanca the **Prime
Minister** flew to Turkey for a meeting with President Inönü.

NEWS CHRONICLE   4th February 1943

WAR OF NERVES

It was frequently rumoured that Hitler had mad fits and that in his
frenzies he ate the carpet. Many people felt that the **Prime Minister's**
journeyings to Cairo, Teheran, Washington, Casablanca and other places,
and his constant changes of attire, helped to foment these frenzies.

"NEVER WAS THERE SUCH A CASE OF THE BITER BITTEN"—MR. CHURCHILL.

The Nazi dachshund found itself harassed by repeated bombing attacks on the Ruhr.

CARTOON BY POY   13th September 1943

THE MYSTERY SOLVED

WINSTON : "*Aha! So this is where you are. Just where you belong!*"

The Prime Minister paid a visit to the Zoo on the day following Mussolini's sudden and mysterious disappearance.

In front of the Allies' victorious drive through Italy, Mussolini resigned his office as *Il Duce* and was put under arrest by the new Italian Cabinet. But he was "rescued" by the Nazis and disappeared for a time ; and it was not until 28th April 1945 that he was recaptured and executed by his fellow-countrymen.

TRIBUNE   24th September 1943

MY !—IT'S WINSTON CHURCHILL

The Prime Minister supported the movement for Basic English.

K

JUST PERFECT HARMONY

HEY ! WINSTON !

Some Labour critics felt that the Prime Minister was preoccupied too
often with the dark days of 1940, when Britain stood alone, and was
slow to help the Russians forward to victory.

After the Cairo Conference, the Prime Minister became ill with pneumonia while on his way to Carthage to consult with General Eisenhower and other Allied commanders about strategical plans for the invasion of Europe in 1944.

. . . — ALENTINE !

Allied landings were made at Anzio in January 1944, and a large-scale attack was launched against German forces defending Rome.

The Prime Minister torn between the ideals of the Atlantic Charter and Conservative Party interests.

THE FIRST ROUND

Questions were asked in Parliament on the comparison between civilian wages and Army pay, many members saying that Army allowances were inadequate. The Government was not prepared at that moment to raise the basic rates in Army pay up to those of industry level. The House divided on the motion, and the Government won. The Hon. Quintin Hogg (now Lord Hailsham) took part in the debate.

KEM'S 'HITLER'S NIGHTMARE'

This cartoon was so popular when it appeared in *Le Petit Parisien* that it was reproduced in 126 different periodicals.

CAIRO REUNION 1955

" REMEMBER THAT MAN—HITLER ? "

A special Air Mail Edition, dated 1st April 1955, was printed inside each copy of the magazine, but the cartoonist's April Fool forecast was not strictly accurate, since Stalin and Roosevelt also died before such a reunion could take place.

READY—STEADY— · · ·

The world was waiting for the expected Allied invasion of Europe.

CHURCHILL—MUCIUS SCAEVOLA AGAINST HIS WILL

When Lars Porsena invaded Rome, Caius Mucius, a Roman patriot, attempted to kill him. Lars Porsena sentenced him to be burnt alive and, to show his contempt for the sentence, Caius Mucius thrust his right hand into a burning brazier until it was consumed. Porsena was so moved by his courage that he pardoned him, and thereafter Mucius received the name Scaevola, meaning left-handed.

The old grave-digger is growing suspicious : " What are those two so pleased about ? I wonder if they imagine that the hole might be for me . . . ?"

Das Schwarze Korps was the newspaper of the S.S.

The Allies were advancing on the fronts in Russia, Burma and Western Europe.

LAST LAP

The " Anvil " operation—the name given to Allied landings in the south of France—was about to be launched ; and the Prime Minister flew to Naples and Corsica to see the start of it. There was renewed hope that the war against Hitler and Mussolini might end this year.

" If I am captured I would much prefer regular execution by beheading in the Tower of London to the farce of a noisy trial in Madison-square."
—Extract from *Mussolini's Diaries*, published in the North Italian Press.

Mussolini was arrested by the new Italian Government on 25th July 1944, a few days before his sixtieth birthday, thus ending his twenty-one years of dictatorship.

PACIFIC INTENTIONS

At the second Quebec Conference in September 1944, further plans were made by the Prime Minister and President Roosevelt for the ultimate defeat of Japan.

MAYBE JOE SHOULD HAVE SENT A PROXY

Stalin was not represented at the Second Quebec Conference. Mr. Earl
Browder was the leading American Communist at this time.

A LITTLE " SWING " MUSIC IN THE KREMLIN

The Prime Minister visited Moscow for conferences with Stalin in October 1944.

" TRUST ME ; I MAY NOT EVEN TOSS YOU "

A so-called Polish National Committee attended the Moscow Conference, and its leader, M. Bierut, said : " We are here to demand on behalf of Poland that Lvov shall belong to Russia. This is the will of the Polish people."

SPEAKING OF UNCONDITIONAL SURRENDER

Another American view of the Moscow Conference. Isolationists in
U.S.A. believed that Uncle Sam was being used by Britain and Russia
for their own ends.

"MY GOODNESS, MY HAPPINESS!"

With apologies to Guinness & Co.

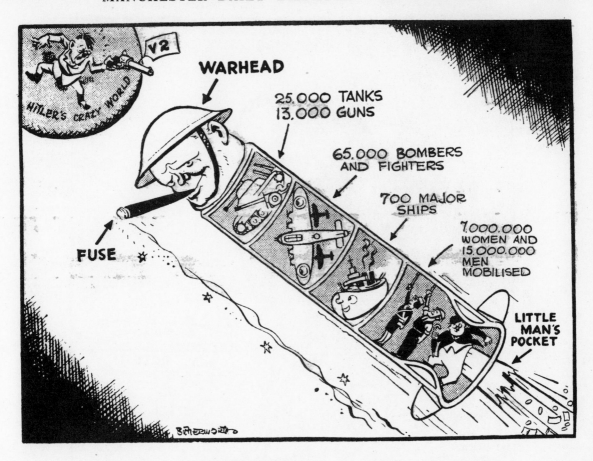

AND WE MEAN V, TOO !

London and south-eastern England were menaced by flying bombs (V1s) and rockets (V2s) at this period.

SEVENTY YEARS ON

The Prime Minister celebrated his seventieth birthday, cheered by the knowledge that the end of the war in Europe seemed to be in sight.

THE GENIE OF THE LAMP

After the Germans were driven out of Greece, the Greeks fought among themselves, and when there seemed danger of Communist supremacy, Britain intervened. On Christmas Eve the Prime Minister and Anthony Eden flew to Athens, which had just been delivered from the Communists, and discussed the situation with Greek leaders. It was arranged that the exiled King should appoint the Greek Archbishop as Regent and that he should form a Government of men of the " best will ".

INTO THE FRYING PAN TO PUT OUT THE FIRE

British troops fought against the Communists in the Civil War in Greece. An American cartoonist's impression of the Prime Minister's visit to Athens.

DESTINY'S CHILD

The Big Four greeted the New Year with renewed hope of an Allied
Military Victory.

TRYING TO DROWN OUT THE WAILS WITH HARMONY

The Russians advanced across Poland, capturing more than a thousand localities with thirty-mile advances in twenty-four hours.

" I WOULDN'T MIND BETTING HE HAD IT BY MISTAKE
FROM A CLOAKROOM ATTENDANT."

The lighter side of the Yalta Conference.

LA FRANCE   February 1945

ONE CAN NEVER BUILD WELL WITHOUT FOUR PILLARS

The French were annoyed because General de Gaulle was not consulted
by the Big Three at the Yalta Conference about the " Peace " after the
war.

WING OR DRUMSTICK ?

At the Yalta Conference Stalin proposed to carve up " the Nazi Bird " — Germany — between the Big Three.

NEWS CHRONICLE   14th March 1945

INTO BATTLE

(THE CONSERVATIVE PARTY CONFERENCE OPENS TODAY)

LOVE ME, LOVE MY DOG

Many people felt that Winston Churchill as the " National Leader "
was overshadowed by the interests of the Conservative Party, and this
issue led to the Conservative defeat in the General Election of 1945, a
few weeks after the surrender of Germany.

Labour critics maintained that the Conservative Party's General Election
programme was too favourable to private enterprise and profits.

TORY DREAM

THEY HAVEN'T CHANGED A BIT !

(THE FIRST OFFICIAL TRAIN BRINGING EVACUEES BACK TO LONDON ARRIVES
TODAY)

Winston Churchill tendered his resignation as Prime Minister of the
National Coalition Government on May 23rd, and formed a " Caretaker
Government " until Parliament dissolved on June 15th.

THE THREE CABALLEROS

The Three Caballeros, a Walt Disney colour cartoon film, was produced
in 1945.

LISTEN AND LEARN

This was the title of a series of broadcast lessons in the Irish language which was running at the time.

A Drawing by Thomas Derrick

The Nazi concentration camps had been opened. The victorious Allies
were confronted by the corpses and brutalities of Belsen, Dachau, etc.
The spectre of malnutrition hovered over Europe.

The final results of the General Election were declared on July 26th.
Both the Prime Minister and Mr. Attlee attended the Potsdam Conference,
which started on July 15th, and when they returned to Britain their
positions had been reversed, Mr. Attlee being the new Prime Minister.

TWO CHURCHILLS

IT TOOK SOME TIME...BUT THEN THE BIG FREE FISHES PULLED TOGETHER !

The end of the story of the Nasty Nazi Fish.

COURIER Winter 1945

THE WESTMINSTER PLAYERS

AND GUILELESS WINNIE SEES WITH DREAD
THE LASKI WOLF HAS REARED HIS HEAD

CARREFOUR, PARIS 27th December 1945

L'An Vu Par EFFEL

AVRIL : LA CONFÈRENCE
DE SAN-FRANCISCO

" Un orfèvre, on n'sait trop
pourquoi, N'alla pas dîner chez
trois autr' bourgeois . . . "

General De Gaulle did not attend
the San-Francisco Conference.

DAILY EXPRESS 16th January 1946

HE IS THE BELLE OF NEW YORK...
THE SUBJECT OF ALL THE TOWN TALK...

He visited America to have talks with President Truman and to receive
the Honorary Degree of Doctor of Law at Miami University. *The Belle
of New York* was a famous musical comedy of the Edwardian era.

THE UNITED STATES OF WINSTON CHURCHILL

Churchill made a controversial speech at Fulton, Missouri, calling for the combining of the military, naval and air strength of the United States and the British Commonwealth. The Soviet regarded it as flagrantly anti-Russian.

FULTON'S FINEST HOUR

The balloon that went up after the Fulton speech ! D. R. Fitzpatrick
is probably the most widely reprinted political cartoonist in the U.S.A.
He almost never caricatures specific personalities, so this cartoon is not
only unique but shows the impact of the Fulton speech.

'BEWARE THE BOGY MAN...'

The *Daily Mail's* reaction to Churchill's speech at Fulton, Missouri.

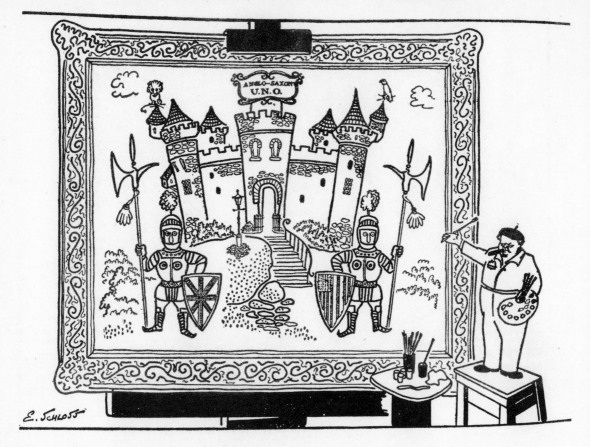

The First General Assembly of the United Nations Organization met in London.

COURTESY AIDS SERVICE

Persia lodged a complaint with the United Nations Security Council, accusing the Soviet Union of violating the Anglo-Soviet-Persian Treaty of 1942 and the Declaration of Teheran.

Posters warning the public to " Keep Death Off The Road " appeared everywhere at this period.

BUBBLES

The Conservative Party believed that the Labour Government would be defeated on the issue of the continued rationing of soap, fats, and bread. " Bubbles " is probably the best-known painting by Sir John Millais.

MARLBOROUGH

LE SANS-CULOTTE

NEWS CHRONICLE 21st November 1946

WALT DISNEY HAS COME TO BRITAIN IN SEARCH
OF NEW CHARACTERS

CHURCHILL'S ARK

Churchill's great aim was a United Europe. In a speech at the Albert Hall in April 1947 he said : " We ourselves are content, in the first instance, to present the idea of United Europe, in which our country will play a decisive part, as a moral, cultural and spiritual conception to which all can rally without being disturbed by divergencies about structure."

DAGBLADET, OSLO   **May 1947**

CHURCHILL : " *Now my main job is to write and paint. If I save England once more it will be just as a hobby.*"

In 1947 he exhibited pictures at the Royal Academy and was writing his *History of the Second World War.*

IT'S THAT MAN AGAIN

Inspired by the B.B.C's famous programme *Itma*, starring Tommy Handley.

ANYTHING HE CAN DO I CAN DO BETTER THAN HIM...

Winston Churchill's speech at the Conservative Party Conference at Brighton was, as usual, full of dynamite.

ACTION, PARIS

27th April 1948

L'OBJECTIF

START OF THE PEACE MARATHON?

Winston Churchill attended the Congress of Europe at the Hague from
7th to 10th May.

OFF WITH THE MOTLEY...

Another view of the Congress of Europe.

" MATCHLESS "

The Labour Party maintained that Winston Churchill would never be able to light the Olympian torch for a United Europe with the Tory Policy as upheld by Lord Woolton.

DAILY HERALD 27th October 1948

" LET BATTLE COMMENCE "

The Labour Government was determined to nationalize the Steel Industry,
but the Conservative Party was violently opposed.

AT EDMONTON, HIS LOVING WIFE
FROM THE BALCONY SPIED
HER TENDER HUSBAND, WOND'RING MUCH
TO SEE HOW HE DID RIDE

William Cowper, *John Gilpin*.

Winston Churchill spoke in support of the Tory candidate, Mr. Hubbard
at a by-election at Edmonton.

IT KEEPS HIM AWAKE

There was a spate of Conservative defeats at by-elections at this period.

RESTORATION COMEDY

"MARK MY WORDS, GENTLEMEN, WE'RE YEARS AHEAD OF OUR TIME."

A number of Restoration plays were revived in the theatre. This fondness
for old modes gave new hope to the Conservatives.

" WOT, STAY IN THE SAME CAGE AS THAT WILD MAN, NOT ME ! "

" AND YOU, MR. CHURCHILL, WHAT HAVE YOU BEEN DOING IN THE LAST
TEN YEARS ? "

The Royal Society of British Artists, who recently elected Giorgio De
Chirico as an Honorary Member, has invited the painter to show in
London one hundred of his pictures, representing his production in the
last ten years. (*The Times*, 4th May 1949.)

ANOTHER STRANGE CRAFT

A DANISH RECONSTRUCTION OF A VIKING SHIP IS ON ITS WAY TO ENGLAND

The Tory Party Conference was held in July.

ATTLEE GET YOUR GUN

THE TRUE-BLUE BOY

Vicky's rendering of "Blue Boy", the famous painting by Thomas Gainsborough.

"I WISH YOU WOULDN'T SMOKE SUCH BIG CIGARS, WINNIE. IT SPOILS THE EFFECT!"

In preparation for the General Election of 1950, the Conservative Party played on the theme that the country was being made bankrupt by the Socialist regime.

DAILY WORKER   2nd March 1950

PEACE PARADE

Winston Churchill was on a short list for the Nobel Peace Prize.

" HE THINKS LIKE A TORY, AND TALKS LIKE A RADICAL, AND THAT'S SO
IMPORTANT NOWADAYS."

Oscar Wilde, *Lady Windermere's Fan*, Act II.

Herbert Morrison and Clement Davies mistrust Winston Churchill's
Liberal-minded speeches.

MIRACLE MAN

In a Parliamentary debate on the Labour Government's Budget Proposals and Economic Survey, Winston Churchill said : " Should the opportunity come when we shall have the chance of presenting our design and policy to the nation, we shall not hesitate to propose definite reductions in expenditure coupled with definite remissions of taxation."

This Russian cartoon entitled *Tcherchill Tchernilnitsa* (the Churchill
Inkpot) is a forced pun. The figure in the foreground is presumably the
diplomatic correspondent of the *Daily Telegraph* (in which the cartoon
was reproduced) and the writer with his tongue out is supposed to be the
representative of the *Daily Mail*. American correspondents in the back-
ground are rushing to dip their pens in the " Dean Acheson Inkpot ".

LOOK OUT! SALOME'S AFTER JOHN'S HEAD AGAIN!

The Schuman Plan, a scheme for pooling French and German production, was not supported by the Labour Government. In a speech at Colchester, Mr. John Strachey, Secretary of State for War, was reported (erroneously, he maintained) as having called the Schuman Plan a " plot " to keep industry in the hands of a few people. His speech was hotly attacked by Winston Churchill and other Members of Parliament.

THEY MISCALCULATED

Headed by Nehru, there was a movement for World Peace, and people
in every country signed peace petitions. Dulles and Acheson are reading
the *Chicago Tribune* and Churchill is reading the *Daily Herald*, the headlines
of which proclaim : "The Peace Movement is doomed to failure."
There were 273,470,566 signatures for peace.

CLOSE LINK

Britain and America accepted the idea of some military revival in Germany.
Russia believed it would be the rebirth of the Nazi Party.

" WHO TOLD YOU WINNIE LIKED CHINA TEA ? "

In a Debate in the House on Britain's Exports to China, which had references to our necessary food imports from that country, the Prime Minister said that Britain's recognition of Communist China was alienating the U.S.A. which had already lost 70,000 men in the Korean war.

KROKODIL, MOSCOW   30 August 1951

" AND THOSE WHO DO NOT AGREE WITH YOUR PROGRAMME, MR. CHURCHILL, WE WILL RELUCTANTLY DRIVE OUT OF OUR PARTY."

This Russian cartoon shows the Labour Party trying to make an alliance with the Conservatives.

" PARTY, PARTY ? I'M INTERESTED IN ONE PARTY ONLY ! "

In Venice the Spanish millionaire, Don Carlos de Bestigui Iturbi, gave a
fantastic party, which received enormous publicity and was attended by
hundreds of celebrities. But Winston Churchill was interested at the time
in only the Conservative Party's prospects at the coming General Election.

THE SHIP OF STATE IF ATTLEE LOSES

(*Above*) AS GILES'S GEORGE DREAMS OF IT.   (*Below*) AS GILES'S VERA DREAMS OF IT.

With a General Election approaching, two of Giles's well-known characters
let their imaginations run riot.

HOT SEAT

When the new Churchill Government took office, their position was
unenviable, and they were faced by a series of crises.

"LOOK YOU! OUR MAN? INDEED TO GOODNESS!"

According to legend, King Edward I presented his new-born child to the Welsh as their Prince.

Sir David Maxwell Fyfe was appointed Home Secretary in the new Government.

" I'M GONNA WASH THAT MAN RIGHT OUTA MY HAIR."

One of the hit tunes from *South Pacific*, the musical play which opened in London on 1st November 1951.

The Conservatives tried to woo Liberal voters, but their overtures were repulsed by Mr. Clement Davies, the Liberal leader.

An impression of the Prime Minister by Kukrinikzi, the Russian artist.

JUST KEEP JOE GUESSING

There was public desire for personal talks between Stalin, Churchill and Truman to endeavour to lessen international tension about the situation in Korea. Churchill visited Truman to discuss what action should be taken should the cease-fire negotiations in Korea fail, and in a speech in Parliament on 30th January about these Anglo-American conversations, he remarked apropos of Britain's recognition of Red China : " As we all know, on both sides of the House, we can recognize many people of whose conduct we do not entirely approve."

CONTROVERSY OVER THE DOME OF DISCOVERY

There had been controversy over the Dome of Discovery in " The Festival of Britain ", which was mainly organized by Mr. Herbert Morrison. A similar controversy now arose regarding the Prime Minister's attitude towards China.

WHAT WITH THE HEAT AND THE JULY NIGHT SKY
VICKY CAN'T SLEEP A WINK

" AND YOU'D BETTER REVIEW THE RELATION OF THE BRITISH GOVERNMENT TO BRITAIN—AND WITH REFERENCE TO SELF - GOVERNMENT ! "

The artist appears to have seen Churchill as another Harry Lauder in this cartoon relating to the Scottish Nationalists, repeated pleas for self-government for Scotland.

CHRISTMAS GLEE CLUB

Although it was seven years since the war finished, rationing was still in force in Britain.

The Prime Minister landed in New York on 5th January and had a long talk with General Eisenhower, the President-elect, before dinner at the home of Mr. Bernard Baruch, the banker.

" I'VE BROUGHT MY PIPE OF PEACE ! "

While in U.S.A. the Prime Minister had talks with President Eisenhower, General McArthur and Mr. Dulles.

FROM PRESIDENT EISENHOWER

General Eisenhower was elected President of the United States. Speculation arose as to whether Chiang Kai-shek's headquarters on Formosa would be used as a base for operations in the Korean war.

DAILY WORKER   28th February 1953

" NO, YOU CAN'T SQUAT IN A TANK TILL WE LEAD THE WORLD IN HOUSES."

The housing shortage was so bad in the years following the war that homeless people " squatted " wherever they could.

" WHAT ! EDEN AND BUTLER AWAY, AND STILL SOMEONE TRYING ON
MY SHOES ! "

Anxiety was felt for the Prime Minister's health when he returned from
holiday in Jamaica and there were suggestions that he should resign the
Premiership.

USING IT AS A BAYONET

Soon after signing the Sudan Agreement with General Neguib, the Egyptian Prime Minister, Britain arrested a number of Sudanese.

" AH, HIS EXCELLENCY SMOKES ONLY HIS OWN
SPECIAL BRAND."

The Western Powers tried to persuade Marshal Tito to join the NATO
group, and he paid a state visit to London to discuss matters. Although
he refused to be wooed into joining any defence plans, he promised that
Yugoslavia would establish a closer alliance with Greece and Turkey.

"NOW, NOW, SIR WINSTON, REMEMBER THE MOTTO OF THE KNIGHTS OF
THE GARTER, 'EVIL TO THOSE WHO EVIL THINK'!"

When Winston Churchill was made a Knight of the Garter, a number of
people thought he would resign the Premiership, and there was a rush
to name his successor.

HONI SOIT QUI MAL Y PENSE

The Rommel Papers had just been published, and attempts were made to whitewash the Nazi General because he had turned anti-Hitler just before his death.

ALTOGETHER : " *I'm the Sheikh of Arabee,*
Your love belongs to me ! "

Britain and America tried to reach an amicable agreement with General
Neguib about the Suez Canal Zone.

RENDEZ-VOUS AUX BERMUDES

" HERE IS THE FRENCH REPRESENTATIVE. BUT WHO IS IT ? "

It was arranged that a Conference would take place in Bermuda between the United States, Britain and France, but France was in the throes of a General Election, and there was doubt as to who would eventually represent her.

It seems that the mice must have been nibbling the power connections at Chequers, too. Winston is considering exchanging his set for an old-fashioned phonograph.

T.V. REPAIRS

Eden
NOT WORKING

MacMillan
HALF WORKING

Butler
ATMOSPHERICS

Monckton
MORE OR LESS

GONE AWAY

Head

Lyttelton

SLIPPING FRAME

OUT OF ORDER

Overlord
STUCK

Fyfe
TECHNICAL HITCH

Crookshank

LOW

POLITICAL T.V. EXHIBITION

The Government was weakened by the illness of Anthony Eden and the absence or illness of other Ministers.

PREPARATIONS FOR A CHARM OFFENSIVE

Upon his death, Stalin was succeeded by Malenkov as Premier of the U.S.S.R. *How to Win Friends and Influence People* is an American best-seller.

THE SPLIT PERSONALITY

The Constitution of British Guiana was suspended by the British Government because it was alleged that the People's Progressive Party, led by Dr. Cheddi Jagan, the Prime Minister, was Communist controlled. A detachment of the Argyll and Sutherland Highlanders was sent to maintain order. Sir Winston had just won the Nobel Prize for Literature, and there were rumours that he might go to Moscow to have peace talks with Mr. Malenkov.

" GOING . . . GOING . . . STILL TO GO."

It was still undecided whether Sir Winston would have talks with the Russian Prime Minister.

" ONE MAN IN HIS TIME PLAYS MANY PARTS "—WITH CONGRATULATIONS
TO SIR WINSTON CHURCHILL, WHO TOMORROW ENTERS HIS 80TH YEAR

The quotation from Jaques' speech in *As You Like It*, beginning " All the
world's a stage ", seems an apt description for Sir Winston ; although
one cannot conceive of his attaining the seventh and last stage "that ends
this strange eventful history ".

LE FIGARO, PARIS 10th December 1953

NOUS AVONS BERMUTÉ

The awaited Conference in Bermuda between Sir Winston, President Eisenhower and M. Joseph Laniel, the French Premier, eventually took place.

LE FIGARO, PARIS 31st December 1953

CONFERÈNCE ULTRA-SECRÈTE AUX BERMUDES

France was still waiting to hear the findings of the Bermuda Conference.

" WHY DON'T YOU MAKE WAY FOR SOMEONE WHO CAN MAKE A BIGGER
IMPRESSION ON THE POLITICAL SCENE ? "

Many people thought that Sir Winston was too old for his office, and a
number of newspapers started a campaign to force him to retire. But the
Prime Minister replied to his critics with such youthful vigour that they
themselves fled ignominiously.

RELUCTANT MOSES

Some Labour Members of Parliament, notably Mr. Aneurin Bevan, who
visited Cairo to discuss the situation with General Neguib, suggested that
the Government " should follow the precedent of Moses and lead our
people out of the land of Egypt immediately "

This cartoon illustrated an article, " What a Role for Churchill ", by
Beverley Baxter. Sir Winston was enthusiastic about Richard Burton's
performance as *Hamlet* and, announcing that Mr. Burton would soon
appear in the role of Coriolanus, Mr. Baxter wrote : " With great respect,
I suggest that Sir Winston has less in common with Hamlet than any man
we know. On the other hand, he is not only like Coriolanus in character
but there is an extraordinary parallel between their careers."

On his way into Town Sir Churchill stopped at a rifle range for a trial shoot with the new Belgian arm, scoring a bull. Asked if he were about to retire on his hundredth birthday he replied "It's a delusion."

LOW'S WILD REPORTER

GRAND OLD EVERGREEN

Sir Winston was so amused at this cartoon that he asked the artist for the original drawing.

MILKING THE SACRED COW

The Conservatives felt that the enormous expenditure on social services
instituted by the Labour Government was a large drain on the Defence
programme.

" WELL, MARK ANTHONY, THE IDES OF MARCH ARE COME . . . "

Trouble between Egypt and Britain still persisted about the Suez Canal Zone.

COMMONS NEWS : *Back benchers seek to restore Cabinet pay cuts—but Churchill says No.*
CUMMING'S VIEW : *Why not pose for adverts ?*

MR JACK SOLOMONS HAVING ANNOUNCED HIS INTENTION OF STANDING FOR PARLIAMENT, **SIR WINSTON CHURCHILL** TAKES TO A PIPE AS HE HAS NO DESIRE TO BE MISTAKEN FOR A FIGHT PROMOTER

NO CIGARS—BY ORDER

Sir Winston did not need to follow Stanley Baldwin's example. Mr. Solomons did not carry out his intention.

FORBIDDEN GAMES

An Italian cartoonist's view of the menace of the " H " bomb

" HOLD IT ! "

France asked America for military aid against the Vietminh rebels in Indo-China. America was willing to give this in order to stem the Communist menace in South-East Asia, but Britain, afraid of precipitating yet another world war, emphatically stated that she would defer military judgments and commitments until after the outcome of the Five-Power Conference at Geneva, which started on March 26th.

FRANCE —
International Motor-racing...

GERMANY —
Ballet: Spectre
de la Rouge...

SWITZERLAND —
World Cup Football:
Eden v. The Rest...

GREAT BRITAIN —
Racing at Westminster

EURODIVISION—A REVIEW OF THIS WEEK'S INTERNATIONAL T.V.

Great Britain—Racing at Westminster

Members of Parliament voted themselves a rise of £500 a year in salary ;
but a number of wealthy Tory M.P.s rebelled against this increase,
saying the country could not afford it. Sir Winston and some other
Members of the Government abstained from voting.

A CHURCHILL L' "ORDINE DELLA GIARRETTIERA"

AUTOSTOP

Queen Elizabeth II invested Sir Winston as a Knight of the Garter in the Chapel at Windsor on 15th June 1954.

NEWS CHRONICLE   23rd June 1954

ANIMAL CRACKERS

" *Act like you can't make out who he's supposed to be — it makes him furious.*"